To Jana~

D1263334

HOW
HEALED
DO YOU WANT
TO BE?

FINDING HOPE AND
WHOLENESS IN A
SHARP-EDGED WORLD

WILLIAM T. "BILL" FARIS, MPC

Bill Faris

ampelōn
PUBLISHING
ampelonpublishing.com

What others are saying about How Healed Do You Want to Be?

"Healing has a thousand angles, and thousands of entry points and exits. Some work, but some leave the patient worse off than when they began the healing process. In *How Healed Do You Want to Be?* Bill Faris presents a way to think about healing within the context of our whole life and invites us to go further."
—**Todd Hunter**, author *Christianity Beyond Belief*
Church Planter, The Anglican Mission in the Americas

"Bill Faris doesn't lead his readers down a path of false hopes, but rather calls them to face off with the possibility that Jesus meant what He said: The kingdom of heaven is at hand, and this kingdom operates by a new economy and new intentions. Bill challenges us to wrestle with a vibrant set of expectations as we look for what God is doing in our lives and in the lives of the people around us. This really is a book about learning to become followers of Jesus who see themselves as God's new and renewed people for the sake of the world."

—**Mike McNichols**, DMin, Director and Adjunct Assistant Professor of Leadership, Fuller Seminary California Coast

"I became aware of Bill's tremendous gift for training laypeople in the art of Christian healing ministry during a series of workshops he gave in 2003. I'm delighted he has developed this practical and engaging guide to help each of us make key decisions about something that is so important to the kind of life we will ultimately live."
—**Mark Edwards**, a Director at CultureROI and
global specialist in technology-based business development

"Bill's personal journey and passionate pursuit of God's best in life, not only engaged me, but confronted and transformed my limited idea of healing. Asking the question, "How healed do I want to be?" is a way of standing for life!"
—**Dan Tocchini**, Founder
The Association For Christian Character Development (ACCD)

How Healed Do You Want to Be?
Copyright ©2009 by William T. "Bill" Faris, MPC

Unless otherwise indicated, Bible quotations are taken from the HOLY BIBLE, NEW INTERNATIONAL VERSION®. Copyright © 1973, 1978, 1984 International Bible Society. Used by permission of Zondervan. All rights reserved.

All rights reserved. No portion of this book may be reproduced or transmitted in any form or by any means, electronic or mechanical, including photocopying, recording, or by any information storage and retrieval system without written permission from the author, except for the inclusion of brief quotations in a review.

ISBN: 978-0-9823286-5-1
Printed in the United States of America
Requests for information should be addressed to:
Ampelon Publishing
PO Box 140675
Boise, ID 83714

To order other Ampelon Publishing products, visit us on the web at:
www.ampelonpublishing.com

Cover & inside design: Jared Swafford — SwingFromTheRafters.com

Printed on paper made from sustainable resources

to my Robin

You are a most remarkable woman, an inspiration to many
and the love of my life

CONTENTS

ACKNOWLEDGEMENTS

The things I have learned about healing and wholeness have come over a lifetime from a variety of sources, but I wish to specially acknowledge the courage and commitment to healing I have encountered in the Vineyard movement thanks to its pioneers, John and Carol Wimber. I also wish to thank my professors and friends at Trinity College of Graduate Studies, Dr. William Heard, Father Joe Scerbo, and Rev. Bob Whitaker for their mentoring and influence.

When it comes to Robin's auto accident and all it brought to our lives, the list of acknowledgements becomes very long, indeed. To our dear church families of the Newport and Crown Valley Vineyards who fought so long and hard for us—you are forever in our hearts. We also acknowledge the countless kindnesses shown to us by Saint Margaret's Episcopal School, Robin's coworkers and friends at Saddleback Hospital, and the many other friends and neighbors who have served us in a thousand-and-one ways.

The medical professionals at Mission Hospital took our family in hand during the biggest crisis of our lives and never let go until Robin was brought back from the brink one step at a time. The list of first-responders, physical and psychological therapists, prayer warriors and chaplains, medical staff and doctors is simple too long to name. You know who you are, however, and we thank you!

Our own extended families have been our heroes and continue to be so. Without their patience, love, attention to detail and perseverance ours story would be much different. I would also like to thank the Furman family for being "family" to us and our kids through these past years. You are all gifts from God and we are forever grateful.

Thanks to Kirk and Annie Kirlin, the folks at ACCD and the

Breakthrough Training, Dr. Steve and Linda Bagley and my Power of Four guys for countless hours of life-shaping interaction, learning and straight talk.

For this writing project—the first of its kind for me—I am blessed to have been led to Jason Chatraw of Ampelon Publishing and, through him, to Cameron Lawrence. Their guidance, feedback and collaboration gave this manuscript wings.

Chris, Colleen, Andrew, Britt, Matthew and JeanneAnn—you are our treasures and the best of our lives. I love you forever.

Finally, I must acknowledge my late and long lost brother, Mike Doyle. Sadly, so much that might have been cannot be. However, thanks to you, Christ became my all-in-all at age 15 and, for that, I owe you everything.

Lord Jesus, it is for You, Your kingdom, Your glory and the honor of Your Name that I release these words to a world that so desperately needs Your saving, healing touch. Thank You, thank You for finding me, giving me life and teaching me how to live by grace in this sharp-edged world.

William "Bill" T. Faris, MPC
Coto de Caza, 2009

0

Introduction

How *Healed Do You Want to Be?* is not just a jazzy book title. It is a serious and timeless question. It asks you to think again about the nature of healing and how deeply you desire to experience it. The question of how healed you want to be can be quantified, but not ignored. In this book you will learn how I, and others, have responded to this provocative question. By doing so, you will be challenged to interact with it for yourself.

The question of how healed you want to be assumes that there is brokenness in this world that, at times, catches us on one or more of its shaper edges. Songwriter Bob Dylan, always the cogent observer of the human condition, captures our problem with the following lyrics from his song *Everything is Broken* on the 1989 album "Oh, Mercy":

> Broken lines, broken strings,
> Broken threads, broken springs,
> Broken idols, broken heads,
> People sleeping in broken beds.
> Ain't no use jiving
> Ain't no use joking
> Everything is broken.
> Seem like every time you stop and turn around
> Something else just hit the ground.

Brokenness, it seems, begets more brokenness. Therefore, it becomes very important for you and me to seek healing for ourselves and for others—now, and for the rest of our lives. And here's the good news: we have not been left alone to do this. Jesus Christ has come to be our Champion, our Savior and our ever-loving Healer. Because of Him and His amazing grace, we no longer have to live as victims in this sharp-edged world. We have, in fact, become the bene-factors of the greatest rescue plan of the ages.

There are those who may question the need for yet another book on the topic of healing. I sympathize. An email I received while writ-ing this book asked why in the world another "theory book" on this subject was needed when, in fact, "we don't heal anyone"—regardless of method or approach. Healing, the writer insisted, is an act of God alone. He will heal according to His own good pleasure; although He "sometimes allows" us to participate with Him. Those several obser-vations may put the issue of healing to bed for that fellow, but it is certainly does not for me.

As a pastor and a trained pastoral counselor, I have spent countless hours walking with people through the challenges, needs and hurts of their lives as a part of my calling in ministry. Through it all, I have learned that we need to have an expansive and inclusive notion of healing if we are going to offer any real hope to people in need; there-fore, we will explore five dimensions of healing in order to better equip you to address your own needs and the needs of others.

I am not ashamed to say I'm a "healing kind of guy." Through the years, I have sought to share healing with people in hospitals, in coun-seling sessions, in private homes, in healing workshops, in the church and even in the marketplace because I truly believe *healing matters.* Furthermore, I have long pursued healing for myself and others because of my conviction that *God cares.* Over the years, I have seen His healing power in action in places as far away as China and as close as my own living room. Everywhere I go, I see the relevance of the healing message to the total human condition: body, soul and spirit.

As we begin, I will take you to the scene of the head-on collision that nearly took the life of my wife in February of 2000. You will learn what that experience taught me, and continues to teach me, about healing. I will also take you to that defining moment in my own life when God first asked the question: "How healed do you want to be?"

By these and other means, I will help you develop a more comprehensive notion of healing—one that I believe will inspire and excite you.

Along the way, I will help you apply some of the things you are learning to your own needs and to the needs of those around you. You will learn about faith, about transformation, about miracles and about the sometimes long, difficult slogs through mystery and pain that is also a part of the healing journey. If you are ready to confront the question that makes up the title of this book, then I urge you to read on. But be forewarned: if you do authentically interact with the question at hand, you will never be the same.

1

Crash

"And... hey, hey, hey! ... Let's be careful out there."
— Sgt. Esterhaus of Hill Street Blues

The cords of death entangled me;
the torrents of destruction overwhelmed me.
The cords of the grave coiled around me;
the snares of death confronted me.
In my distress I called to the LORD;
I cried to my God for help.
From his temple he heard my voice;
My cry came before him, into his ears.
— Psalm 18:4-6

The wipers of our family minivan cycled furiously as the winter rain came down in sheets. Robin gripped the wheel tightly as she peered through the windshield at the storm-drenched road. She had made this part of the trip home from our children's school many times before. The gentle grade rose up through the old ranch land to the top of the hill where 8,000 new homes were under construction.

Our teenage son Andrew sat next to his mom in the front passenger seat while the stereo competed with the thrumming rain. Behind him our 3-year-old daughter was buckled securely into her child safety seat. It had been raining hard for several days and the roads were slick and treacherous. Behind the wheel, Robin was still feeling a little badly about having to refuse to include one of the neighbor kids in that day's ride home from school. The little girl was without her car seat, however, and that was one rule Robin would not break. As she was thinking about these things, she didn't notice the pickup truck coming from the opposite direction as it gained speed, moving down the hill away from the new construction area. She never even saw it slide sideways across the four-lane road and directly into her path, hydroplaning out of control.

In only a second it was over—the mangled vehicles wrapped around each other, steam hissing from the wreckage and dissipating into the falling rain. In the pickup truck, the passenger was already dead on the scene and the driver badly injured. In our family's vehicle, the range of injury was unbelievably broad. Andrew had some relatively minor hurts, while Jeanne Ann had been totally spared. Robin's injuries, however, were devastating.

At the time of the impact, I was busy at home. A friend stopped by to show me the new business cards and stationery designed for our new church start-up. How could I have ever guessed that as we sat there imagining the future, half of my family was en route to the local trauma center? I would know nothing of this until I happened to check my phone messages. The unexpected one from Mission Hospital nearly took my breath away. The sober voice on the recording urged me to come right away—my family had been in a terrible accident.

I prayed as I drove, trying my best to imagine what I would find when I got to my destination. Whatever it was, I knew our lives would never be the same.

★ ★ ★ ★ ★

Four days before the accident our family had been caught up in a very different kind of excitement. On that happy Sunday night, we stood side-by-side before the leaders of our church at a commissioning service in our honor. The Newport Vineyard had been our church home for 10 years and our ties there were strong. Well-wishers and dear friends joined our senior pastor and his wife in praying for God's blessings over us as we prepared to answer a call to begin a new church near our home. After months of preparation, our launch day had finally arrived.

Now, after less than a week had passed, I walked through the hospital doors on a different kind of mission—a mission to find out what had happened to my family. A host of sympathetic faces watched as nurses led me deep into the back rooms of the hospital. At last I was able to see my daughter. She was lying on an examination table with a plastic stabilization yoke around her shoulders and neck. Almost instantly, the medical staff assured me the yoke was purely a precaution and could soon be taken off. Jeanne Ann was shaken, but fine. Now, where were my wife and son?

Andrew, it turned out, had been admitted to a hospital room upstairs. Again, the medical personnel quickly assured me that, although he had some lacerations and a broken thumb, he was fine and resting well. "Thank God," I sighed.

When I asked what had happened to Robin the mood changed. Suddenly things got a lot more serious. People were asking me if I'd like to sit down. Time slowed and voices blurred as several doctors and specialists explained what had happened to my wife—how they intended to help her, if they could.

"She's in surgery right now," I was told. "And she won't be out of the recovery room until morning. At that time, they'll take her to the Intensive Care Unit." This would turn out to be the first of a number of surgeries Robin would undergo.

The accident had produced a tremendous number of broken bones—about 50 fractures in all. Her hip was in six pieces and her left elbow in about 20. All her toes were broken and both knee caps, too. But that was not all. Robin had also suffered serious head injuries. Her brain stem was bleeding. Doctors also monitored two other intercranial bleeds. A nine-inch gash on the left side of her head would need stitches. These things concerned the doctors most. Our family, it seemed, had just been caught on one of life's sharper edges.

Have you ever been in one of those situations in life where everything around you seemed to shout, *You are not in control!?* I was not in control. The medical team would do its best, but no one could predict the outcome. As the wee hours of morning sluggishly came and went, I waited for any news about Robin. I prayed. I hoped. I admitted that things were out of my hands. *In my distress I called to the LORD; I cried to my God for help. From his temple he heard my voice; My cry came before him, into his ears.*

* * * * *

Morning came and I was finally able to visit Robin. She appeared battered and unnaturally swollen—her beautiful blonde hair partially shaved and her eyes tightly shut. As she lay there, the mechanical rhythms of a respirator reminded me that she needed assistance to breathe properly. Medical equipment and monitors of various sorts were banked around her, including one piece of equipment that constantly monitored the pressure inside her skull.

By now, many friends and family members joined together both on the hospital property and offsite to pray and show solidarity with our family. I spent as much time as I could at Robin's bedside, quietly praying over her and laying my hands upon her as an act of healing. The doctors had their job, I figured. I had mine.

In a way, it seemed ironic to pray so intensely for the healing of my wife, considering how often we had prayed for so many others in days gone by. From our earliest beginnings as a couple, we had been involved with churches that embraced the Holy Spirit's supernatural gift of healing ministry. Eventually, we became involved in the rapidly-growing Vineyard movement—known for its emphasis on contemporary worship music and healing prayer ministry. We loved being a part of our new church home, the Anaheim Vineyard, and its pastor, John Wimber.

Robin and I were attracted to the training sessions in healing prayer ministry offered at our new church home. Before long we joined a trained prayer team that had been put together to support John Wimber as he conducted large-scale healing conferences in England. We found these environments to be profoundly alive with faith and divine power, and we were amazed at how many opportunities we had to pray for others.

Once at a meeting in Sheffield, England, Robin placed her hand in prayer on the ear of a strapping young Irishman. A moment before, he told us of the high level of hearing loss he had suffered in one ear due to an explosion in his violence-rocked homeland. After praying with him a few moments, we asked him if there had been any change. To our astonishment and joy, his hearing had returned to normal! Now, Robin—who had participated in miracles performed by God for the sake of others—was in need of a miracle of her own.

The Gift of Fight

As the first days of Robin's long hospital stay wound on, I became aware of something I did not expect—something I call *the gift of fight*. I suppose others might just call it "faith," but I much prefer the term "fight" because that's what it felt like inside of me. Somehow, without being aware of it, I had turned into a spiritual warrior committed to nothing less than Robin's complete recovery. There had been plenty of trauma, terror, injury and mystery in those early weeks and no one would have blamed me for succumbing to at least some despair. But I did not feel despairing. I felt *fight*. It was certainly not because I am some sort of hero with nerves of steel; rather, it seemed to me that God had given me some kind of amazing unction to fight for her from the beginning.

I experienced the gift of fight as different from the so-called "fight-or-flight" response you sometimes hear about. The latter is some sort of adrenaline-fueled power surge that kicks in during a crisis only to recede again. By contrast, the gift of fight arose in me as a quiet ferocity that found expression as I prayed while driving to the hospital that first rain-soaked evening. Everything inside of me seemed alive with defiance. Angrily, I growled out the words, "OH, NO YOU DON'T!" over and over again, as if the devil himself could hear me.

After all, had we not just been sent out to fulfill a call from God to begin a new church? And wasn't there something about this accident that seemed like an attempt by the enemy to derail our lives, our dreams and our mission? It was as if something inside me was rising up and declaring, *I'm not having any of this.* I felt as if my wife's life and well being had somehow become the frontlines of an invisible war between heaven and hell, and there was only one outcome I could live with and that was *victory*—for Robin and our family, our church and the kingdom of God. This was the engine that drove the mysterious gift of fight, or faith, or whatever it was that had me in its holy grip. And most amazing of all, it lasted for three solid years.

As the news of Robin's condition rolled in and the various surgeries and treatments came and went, the gift of fight remained. It kept me in an almost ceaseless undertone of prayer. It also helped me provide and maintain as much stability as possible for my children as we attempted to cope with the crisis that had overtaken our home. The gift of fight fueled a number of quiet bedside vigils. It kept me sane as I watched my wife struggle with the inevitable ups and downs that came with such severe injuries. And, last of all, the gift of fight expressed itself in a determination to plant the flag of our new church that March 25th—the day Robin and I had originally chosen before the unimaginable happened.

This inner fight actually caused some of the nurses in the Intensive Care Unit to feel concern. Quietly, they questioned my sisters-in-law as to whether or not I was coping. I think they sincerely mistook my resolve for denial. But even to my own surprise, I danced very little with denial or despair, constantly aware what was at stake at every point. However, this gift of fight within me kept pushing my energy outward—away from myself and toward my family. It also helped me identify some of the more subtle ways God was present and working in and around our tragic situation. Somehow, I knew He was there using all the things we were going through to accomplish His divine purposes.

Can Your Relate?

Perhaps you can relate to the life-shaking experience I have just described. It may be that you or your loved ones have had to endure a "sudden onset" crisis such as an accident, a layoff or an act of violence. Or maybe you are still reeling from a divorce, the death of a child, the collapse of a dream or the aftermath of sexual abuse. You may even be engaged in a long-term struggle with addiction, severe loneliness, chronic depression, overwhelming fear, persistent doubts, an eating disorder or the loss of your will to live. All of these things profoundly impact our bodies, oppress our souls and break our hearts. They also often severely test our faith in God. Perhaps the Psalm-writer's prayer could easily be the prayer of your own heart:

> Be merciful to me, LORD, for I am faint;
> O LORD, heal me, for my bones are in agony.
> My soul is in anguish. How long, O LORD, how long?
> Turn, O LORD, and deliver me;
> save me because of your unfailing love.
>
> — Psalm 6:2-4

There are times all of us can identify with those cries for healing, mercy and relief. It's a sharp-edged world and people get hurt—people like me, you, and the godly man who wrote that Psalm. Where can we find healing, wholeness and hope? How will we recognize it when it comes? Will our rescue come quickly or will the way out of the valley be long and difficult—or even impossible?

Like me, you have had to confront such questions in your life—and we all need healing. Together, we will learn to think more comprehensively about healing by becoming better acquainted with its five dimensions. This will help you develop a "road map" you can use to guide you more specifically on your journey towards wholeness. You'll also be learning more about God's healing grace—what it is and how it works—so that your faith will grow and your hope increase. The new faith and hope you will gain can then fuel your vision of what is possible concerning your own healing and the healing of others.

If you are ready to begin, then come with me in the next chapter to a most remarkable place and time. You will hear for yourself the gateway question that changed a broken man's life and has the power to change your own life, too: *Do you want to be healed?*

2

Mercy

I was standin' in a bar and watchin' all the people there,
Oh the loneliness in this world, you know it's just not fair.
Love and mercy is what you need tonight,
So love and mercy to you and your friends tonight.

— Brian Wilson, *Love and Mercy*

On the east side of Old Jerusalem, there was once a pool of water called Bethesda. Its name means *House of Mercy*, although some people called it "the Sheep Pool". At the time of Jesus, the Pool of Bethesda was a crowded place where desperate people gathered in great numbers. Its five porch areas (*porticos*) were clogged with the sick, lame and outcast—sad souls in extreme need. In the center of the area, divided in two parts, was the spring-fed pool that drew crowds to its waters. People said there were times when miracles happened there.

We can only imagine the crush, din and smell of the scene around the pool. Had you come by for a look, nothing about Bethesda would have made you want to stay—not unless you were in serious need of a miracle. In that case, you would do what everyone else did: carve out a spot as close as possible to the water's edge and wait. Legend had it that, every so often, the Angel of the Lord would come to stir the pool. The first person to step into the freshly troubled water would be made well, no matter what his condition. (see John 5:4)

In his gospel, the Apostle John takes us to this remarkable setting in order to spotlight the experience of a particular man who interacts with Jesus there. We don't know much about the man's background, not even his name. But we do know that he had been paralyzed for 38 years. It is also clear that he was alone with no one to help him win the race for a miracle cure. I doubt you could have found a more pitiful, hopeless case in Bethesda on the day Jesus arrived for a visit.

There He was, navigating the crowded *porticos* with characteristic confidence, kindness and authority—picking His way through the throng. He was on a mission known only to Himself, one that now brought Him before the paralyzed man. The handicapped man must have wondered why he had suddenly become the focus of a stranger's attention. Jesus had come to ask him a question. It was a direct question, one that possibly sounded rude: "Do you want to be healed?"

Sam's Story

Some years ago, while I was on the staff of a large church, Sam came to see me for counseling. He thought I might be able to help him with some things that were on his mind.

On the surface, his life appeared to be nicely put together. He had an active faith, a lovely and devoted wife, two fine young children, a steady job and a nice suburban home. But smoldering beneath the surface was a secret powerful enough to take away his many blessings: Sam was a weekend binge drinker. And at the time of our meeting, his drinking had begun to seriously interfere with the rest of his life. But none of this had anything to do with why he wanted to speak with me. He had come to complain.

Sam was angry. Among other things, he was angry about how badly things were going at work. He was frustrated by what he felt was wrong with the church. And he was upset with his wife who he accused of being a constant nag. In fact, Sam had a long list of things that needed to change if he was ever going to have the life he deserved. As he went through the list, he never once mentioned his drinking problem. It wasn't until his wife (the "nag") joined us for an appointment that I heard about the true source of Sam's woes.

Soon after we began talking, Sam's wife told me about his drinking problem and the troubling behaviors that went with it. As she went into detail, Sam became visibly uncomfortable. Recently, she said, things had gotten to the point where he would load their kids into his truck and drive around town while under the influence. Sam, of course, played this down. Although his wife was sick with concern about the whole situation, he merely shook his head and said she had it all wrong.

Now that Sam's secret was out, he chose to respond by blaming others for his problems. He faulted his wife's nagging, stresses at work, and pointed out how disappointed he was in the Christian 12-step recovery group he had tried out once or twice. After our meeting was over, Sam and I only saw each other a couple more times. By then, he was no longer interested in my counsel, and attempts to reach out to him were ignored. Like everyone and everything else in Sam's life, I had also let him down.

I was shocked several months later to find Sam at the door of our church waiting to speak with me. It was a hot day and he looked over-heated, unshaven and disheveled. Despite his appearance, I instantly noticed something different about him. "What's going on?" I asked, inviting him inside.

The night before, Sam and his wife had gotten into another one of their heated conflicts about his drinking. Agitated and angry, he eventually walked out of the house, jumped into his truck and drove away—leaving his wife and kids behind. Not knowing where else to go, he picked out an empty parking lot several miles away and pulled in. As he sat there alone in the dark, frustrated and upset, it began to dawn on him why he was there. Rather than enjoying a pleasant evening at home with the people he loved, his choice to continue drinking had landed him in a lonely parking lot. The penny, as they say, had finally dropped. Sam was starting to get it.

This time, instead of blaming others, Sam found the courage to push through his anger and look at himself. He didn't like what he saw. For the next several hours, he did some serious thinking and praying about the kind of life he wanted to live and the changes he would need to make to get there. He realized that everything he loved was at stake. It was his moment of truth.

Sam spent the rest of that night in his truck. The next morning, he left it behind and began his long walk to the church. When I asked him if he wanted me to give him a lift back to his truck, he said no. He was on his way to get help at the "Charlie Street House"—a residential alcohol recovery program a few blocks away. He was only stopping by to let men know what had happened to him and to solicit my prayers and support as his pastor. Before heading back out into the hot outdoors to finish his long walk that day, Sam said one last thing. "Pastor Bill, I'm going to change my life *if it kills me.*" With that, he was on his way.

Sam did check in to the recovery program that day and went on to complete the residential portion before moving back home to live with his family. In the meantime, they continued to worship at our church together. We took time to check in with one another regularly, often recalling the moment of truth that brought him by the church on that all-important day. We also talked about the ways we both believed God would use his experiences to bring benefit to others. I still smile when I think of the way Sam came to answer that most important healing question.

A Story That Hits Home

Feelings of helplessness are not confined to any time or place but are as real to a man like Sam, alone and distraught in his truck, as they were to the lame man by the miracle pool. We may have done our best to get close to the hope we need, only to end up feeling as if we can't break through. If our friends could help us, we know they would. But sometimes even they cannot provide that all-important push into the healing waters. Like the man at Bethesda, we may feel alone, paralyzed and without prospects.

I was feeling a lot like that about 10 years before Robin's accident. Unlike the accident, this earlier struggle overtook my life like a slow drip of deepening difficulty. Circumstances had been pushing Robin and me into a thickening cloud of depression that had begun to seriously disrupt our lives. I tried hard to believe that things would soon get better, but it was getting more and more difficult to do.

Have you ever wrestled with that powerful, invisible enemy called *despair?* Besides pulling you ever lower into its own negative energy, despair has a way of amplifying every other negative emotion, experience or perception you have. It ends up feeling as though someone let all the air out of your soul.

That's what life was like for us during those dark days. I had my own set of struggles, but I was becoming more and more concerned that Robin was losing her ability to cope. Like the man languishing by Bethesda's pool, I needed a life-changing encounter with the Lord. What I didn't know was how close I was to having one.

It happened one morning as I retreated to the familiar comfort of my cozy living room sofa. I would go there each day to read my Bible and pray with varying success. When I opened my Bible that day to John, chapter five, I soon became captivated by the story of the man at the pool of Bethesda.

When I got to the part where Jesus asks the crippled man, "Do you want to be healed?" I paused. Something about that question ran against the grain of how I pictured Jesus behaving around hurting people. Although the Gospels describe a number of occasions when Jesus heals entire crowds of troubled, handicapped and diseased people, something different happens that day at Bethesda. Jesus bypasses dozens of needy people in order to place His focus on just one man. And instead of the man coming to Jesus to ask for healing, Jesus is the One to initiate.

But of all the things that caught my eye that day, nothing stood out more than the question Jesus poses: *"Do you want to be healed?"* Why would He speak so bluntly to such an unfortunate man? Couldn't He see that the fellow was hoping for a miracle, not an interrogation?

Rather than respond directly to Jesus' simple question, the man launches into a description of the obstacles he faces. *"Sir,"* the invalid replied, *"I have no one to help me into the pool when the water is stirred. While I am trying to get in, someone else goes down ahead of me"* (John 5:7).

Frankly, it wasn't too hard for me to understand why the poor guy went there. After 38 years in his condition, Jesus' question might simply have gotten by him; that is a long time to go through life dependent on the pity of others. It's a long time to wrestle with thoughts about whether your life would ever be anything other than what it had always been—a protracted struggle to survive. Maybe he really didn't know what he wanted. Or maybe he had already decided to give up hope.

As I sat there with my Bible in my lap, something began to dawn on me: *I am this crippled man!* Of course that's not to say that I shared his besetting physical handicaps. Still there was something about his helplessness, frustration and aloneness that I could very much relate to. Like him, I knew I could not change my own life. Like him, I felt defined by my limitations. And like him, I was in need of someone who could interrupt my decline and give me a reason to hope. It was at that moment that I heard the Lord's timeless question leap across the ages to confront me: *Bill, do you want to be healed?*

Did I want to be *healed*? Healed of *what* and *how*? But I already knew the answer. Yes, I wanted to be healed. I want to be healed of my hopelessness, small-mindedness, fears and unbelief. My answer would have to be "yes!" It was the only response I could imagine living with. I lifted my eyes brimming with tears toward heaven. I gave the Lord *my* answer to His deeply poignant question: "Yes, Lord," I said aloud, "I want to be healed."

Before confronting that question and answering it for myself, I had the attitude of a long-time invalid. But afterward, my perspective started to shift. Instead of focusing on the outward things I wanted God to remove, change or smooth out, I was suddenly aware that He was right there with me, asking me about the wholeness of my being—mind, body, soul and spirit. My "yes" answer to His piercing question did not cause the heavens to quake or the earth to tremble beneath me. There were no shafts of light suddenly streaming through my window, or angelic songs of glory in the air. Nevertheless, I knew something very significant had just taken place in my life. I wonder—how you will see your life differently after you interact with this same, timeless question?

The Journey Begins

"Do you want to be healed?" What is happening to you right now

as you read these words? How do you see your situation in light of Jesus' question? Do you focus your attention on the people, problems and circumstances that stand in the way of the wholeness you long for? Do you blame them for your present situation, whatever it may be? If so, you must feel as powerless as the man at Bethesda. Like him, you are well acquainted with your limitations and the details of the obstacles you face. You may even be convinced that your only hope for change is for someone or something else around you to change—things you can't control. It is a diminishing way to live.

Indeed, there is a world of possible things we might want as we wait alone by our miracle pools. Maybe we want an instant solution to our most perplexing problems. Or perhaps we want those we blame for our misery to change and apologize for all the pain they cause. We may want relief, fun, success or love. Maybe we want more of some things and less of others: a new body, a new deal or a new partner; less debt, less pain and less struggles. We may have headaches, heartaches and toothaches—*but do we want to be healed?*

If you can sincerely answer "yes", a customized, God-designed path toward wholeness begins. The first step ahead takes place when we surrender our inborn desire to control the things and people around us to God and accept His will for our lives. From then on, we are liberated to engage the journey God planned and designed for us—the one that will bring us to wholeness.

Of course, with God in control, our circumstances may suddenly change in miraculous ways. That's what happened to the man at Bethesda, as we shall soon see. But that is not up to us. God is in charge of the miracle department, while we are in charge of the keep-saying-yes-to-Him department. This means we have to learn to resist the temptation to call our own shots by self-managing our sin, brokenness, infirmities and pain. If we do somehow return to old, familiar patterns, we can be assured that He is always ready to receive our repentance and put us back on the healing path.

A "yes" answer to the question is not required. We can stall, dodge, ignore or neglect our moment of truth (at least for a while). We can respond by turning down God's gracious healing offer with a simple "No thanks." But however we respond, it is important to understand that the position we take concerning this key question will powerfully affect the kind of life we will come to lead.

Notice, now, that Someone has taken an interest in you. He is standing close by you, waiting patiently for you to answer His question. He is not asking you what is wrong (He already knows). He's asking if *you* want to be different. Do you just want *things* to change or do you want *you* to change—do you want to become whole?

Is your focus shifting now? Instead of continuing to pin your hopes on improved circumstances, a better deal, a measure of relief, a way out of the mess you're in, or the answers to your "why me" questions, are you now looking within? Can you hear that question as it reverberates once again through your soul: *"Do you want to be healed?"* I urge you to put this book down now and give the Lord *your* answer.

3

Choice

You've got to kick at the darkness 'till it bleeds daylight.

— Bruce Cockburn, songwriter

As a boy growing up in Arizona, my first memory of swimming in the ocean remains vivid. I was just a kid visiting California with my family when I learned there are four things about the beach that you must understand if you want to enjoy the Pacific—or even survive it. First, you must understand the tides, including the potential danger of a riptide. Second, you must be aware of the saltiness of the water (imagine the taste of eating a handful of salt!). Next, you must realize that slimy strands of loose seaweed sometimes wrap around your ankles as you wade into the surf. Kids often mistake these for the unpleasant parts of an octopus, jellyfish or giant squid. And finally, you must understand the nature of waves.

When it comes to waves, it is important to understand how they come at you, one after the other, in a sequence called a "set". The fastest way to appreciate this phenomenon is to push your head through one freshly foaming wave after it has slammed you silly just in time to get hammered by the next one (see the preceding note regarding salt overload).

In a spiritual kind of way, that's what happened to me as I sat on my sofa with my Bible open to the book of John. I realized that the Spirit of God also comes in waves.

That day, while still caught up in saying "yes" to the Lord's healing work in my life, I was hit by a second wave of spiritual impact in the form of another question—a follow-up question just as arresting as the first one. It was simply this: *"How healed do you want to be?"*

"What?" I said aloud, "There's a choice?"

But of course, I knew there was. Hadn't I seen people make choices about the amount of healing they would experience in their lives? Hadn't I made such choices myself?

Reminded of Mike

The most powerful healing choices I made in my life all began as spiritual ones. Although raised in a religious home, it wasn't until I was 15 years old that I first surrendered my life to Jesus Christ. Those were the heady days of what came to be known as the Jesus Movement in America—a remarkable period in youth culture during which tens of thousands of young people embraced the Bible, preached the Gospel, and testified to anyone within reach that they had become "born again" followers of Jesus.

It was a time when miracles happened everywhere, it seemed. Our faith was high and our mission clear: don't let *anyone* miss a chance to get to know Jesus! Much of the established church structures and denominations were caught by surprise as hordes of long-haired, Bible-toting youth appeared out of nowhere. As a result, a wide variety of new groups and Christian movements emerged, each of them with a life of its own. By and large, members of these groups took the Bible literally and their faith seriously. You might say we treated the Book of Acts as a how-to manual, rather than merely an inspired record of the past.

Before long, I was baptized in a nearby river and, a few weeks later, experienced the so-called "baptism of the Holy Spirit" through the laying on of hands. This was my gateway to the supernatural gifts of the Spirit. Speaking in tongues, prophecy and divine healing—this was powerful stuff for a sophomore in high school, and I loved every minute of it. I was surrounded by a whole new tribe of young people my age and older. These new friends shared my passion for God, love of worship and Bible study, and the desire to tell others about what we had found in Jesus. Our informal collection of young *Jesus freaks* was led by a compelling 19-year-old hippie preacher named Mike.

Mike experienced a remarkable conversion only a few years earlier. Although he had graduated from high school, Mike had no formal college or theological training. But whatever he lacked in training, he made up for in charisma. He was God's own pied piper, and I was his number one fan. Over time, the number of those influenced by Mike began to swell. We sometimes joked that, back then, you could sneeze people into the Kingdom of God.

As for me, Mike was part big brother, part spiritual guru. I imitated everything about him. He taught me how to study and teach the Bible, and how to share my faith. I hitchhiked with Mike to visit some of the new Christian coffeehouses that had opened around town. We ate day-old donuts, listened to Christian music and shared fellowship with whatever "brothers and sisters" we might meet. Mike was my main man.

While I was still in high school, Mike married. His new wife was one of our group's female leaders and all of us approved of their union. Before long, they had set up their new home near my school. This made it easy for me to become a rather relentless drop-in pest, I'm afraid. Meanwhile, things began to change for our group. Little-by-little we were becoming aligned with the rapidly-growing "charismatic movement" that swept through the American church in the 1970s. In contrast to the Jesus Movement, during which great numbers of previously unchurched youth became committed to Christ, the so-called "Charismatics" were typically "Spirit-renewed" Christians from mainline denominational backgrounds. In increasing numbers, they explored such lively expressions of faith as tongue-speaking, healing prayer ministry and contemporary worship music in small prayer groups, large conferences and in a growing number of churches.

By the time I was 18, I was ready to leave Phoenix behind in order to attend a new Bible School in California. It was my hope to become a full-time pastor one day, perhaps in one of the new charismatic-styled churches springing up everywhere. Mike supported my move further west and we stayed connected through letters and phone calls. By mid-1976, I finished my Bible School degree and married Robin that summer. Mike was the best man in our wedding.

A couple of years later, Mike and his family, which now included three children, were moving to California! It was difficult to arrange visits after the move, but we still managed to find time to enjoy one another's company. Mike had accepted a position in a small church as an assistant pastor working with youth. It felt gratifying to see him back in the saddle of church leadership. I hoped this would be the beginning of a new chapter in Mike's ministry. How could I have known that he was about to lose it—his faith, family and eventually his life?

I first learned Mike was in trouble when his wife called me in tears one day to tell me he had left their family. The next months and years unfolded like bad dream as I watched my spiritual big brother conceal his whereabouts from his wife and kids and start a new life with another woman. There was a long period of time when Mike's family had no idea where to find him. Later, after he resurfaced, he began working sales jobs by day and playing in country-rock bar bands at night. For some reason, the man I once highly regarded was relentlessly reinventing himself—even scuttling all associations with his former life and family.

After several failed attempts, I was finally able to arrange a lunch meeting with Mike. It was hard for us to speak freely since we shared so little in common anymore. But, eventually, I asked him the questions that had been haunting me.

"Why are you doing this—living like you are? What's happened to you? What's happened to your faith?"

All he could say in reply was, "I'm just being stupid."

Eleven years after leaving his family to begin his new life, Mike finally received word that his divorce was finalized. A couple of days later, Mike died. The news hit me like a sledgehammer.

One afternoon, Mike had come in from mowing his lawn to enjoy a cold drink in his kitchen. Suddenly, he was overcome by a massive heart attack and fell to the floor where, a moment or two later, he breathed his last, dead at age 44. The following week, I stood in a small, crowded chapel and preached Mike's funeral.

That afternoon, I listened as a wide variety of people got up to say a few words about Mike. Some spoke of how he had led them to Christ, taught them the basics of following Jesus and profoundly influenced the rest of their lives. Others paid tribute to Mike the salesman and country-rock bar musician who "loved his beer and a shot." An open casket bearing Mike's remains had been placed in the center of the platform area only a few feet from where I stood and directed the service.

Although there is much about that day that is still a blur to me, one moment stands out as crisp, clear and sharp as broken glass. One of Mike's daughters read a letter written the night before by his young son. Addressed to his dad, the letter read in part: "It's been really interesting listening to all these people tell stories about you these past several days. They tell me I have eyes like yours and your stubby fingers, too. I wouldn't know because I don't remember you at all." It was all I could do to keep my composure and continue the service.

What had happened to my friend, my brother, my spiritual leader? When did the disease that collapsed his soul and broke the hearts of his children first begin? What were the signs and symptoms of its onset? Wasn't Mike a man who had been miraculously transformed? Why did he choose to let it all go? Was it because only we can choose how healed we want to be?

Looking for More

For years, I tucked away the question in my soul: "How healed do you want to be?" The dismally dark days surrounding my first encounter with that question eventually passed as better days arrived at last. Robin was enjoying her dream job as a labor and delivery nurse in a state-of-the-art hospital, and I had been invited to join a first-rate church staff as an assistant pastor. Our growing children kept us busy at home and our vocational lives were meaningful and challenging. We felt truly blessed and hopeful about the future. Still, in my heart I knew God didn't want me to settle simply because life had improved. It was time to move forward and grow.

I decided to voluntarily resume counseling with a professional Christian therapist. She had helped me a great deal during my "sofa days" of depressing difficulty. This time, however, I came back to explore, to grow and deepen my grasp on the person God was making me to be. As time went on, I could see how our work together was beginning to bear fruit in my spiritual life, ministry and my family relationships.

At church, the scope of my ministry was widening. Although I continued to participate in healing prayer ministry and pastoral counseling, I was also put in charge of the food and clothing pantry outreach of our church. Later, I was asked to develop a new ministry for single adults that included a weekly meeting on Sunday and a midweek home group fellowship. All of these opportunities stretched me in new ways.

I felt a deepening desire to become better equipped to address the various needs I was encountering. So, when I learned of a nearby Christ-centered training institution that offered a graduate degree in pastoral counseling I was ecstatic. My hope was to develop an expanded, holistic and enriched model of healing that I could employ in my life and ministry. I hoped that by doing so I would increase my effectiveness as a pastor and grow personally at the same time.

It was about mid-way through this program that I had another unexpected moment of truth brought on by another question. This time, it was a professor doing the asking. When I first heard it, I figured it would be easy to answer—*a real slam dunk,* I thought. Turning to the class, he paused to ask us: "What is your notion of healing?"

For a moment, his words seemed to hang in the air as my fellow students and I silently considered how to supply a thoughtful response. What is my notion of healing? I thought to myself. *Everyone knows what healing is. It's... it's... well, it's when things that are sick or broken get better, or... something like that.* I was beginning to see why he asked us such an "easy" question.

There was something about this question stayed with me long after the class had concluded. It took me back to the wonder I had felt years before when I first began to prayerfully ponder the life-changing text from John's gospel alone in my living room. When I heard the words, "What is your notion of healing?", I found myself struggling to give definition to what it is that the word *healing* actually describes. What is *your* notion of healing?

A Hardworking Word

If you're like me, working with this question makes you realize how much we ask of that little word *healing*. There are some times we use it to describe bodily repairs or improvements: "Charles broke his arm last month, but it's *healed* now." Other times, we talk about the need to heal a relationship, an emotional wound or a spiritual condition: "Thank God, Bobby and Sandy were able to *heal* their troubled marriage." It is obvious that some healings are outward and visible while others require special effort, spiritual discernment or medical tests to observe. There are healings that take place rapidly—miraculously, even—while others call for an extended period of time. Given the complexity of the human experience, our notion of healing must not be fixed, but elastic and inclusive.

The idea that life has its hurts is nothing new. In this world you will have trouble, Jesus warned. And these troubles of mind, body and spirit come in all shapes and sizes. If you are alive and breathing on Planet Earth, troubles, injuries, losses and wounds come with the territory. What's more, they are not distributed "fairly" or evenly.

Take Robin, for example. She suffered over 50 bone fractures in the crash, while some people never break one. On the other hand, Robin's childhood memories are largely happy and pleasant, while many other people endured childhoods that left them with brutal interior pain. But one thing is certain: everyone dances with pain in some way and at some time in their life. Isn't it about time we danced with healing, too?

Since there are so many kinds of troubles, injuries and wounds, there must also be many kinds of healing. And if illnesses, brokenness and dysfunctions often take time to become detectable, we shouldn't be surprised to find that healing takes time, too. On the surface level, symptomatic change is relatively easy to chart. But when it comes to those deeper, subterranean works of grace, how do we detect progress? I believe it takes patience, faith and understanding to discern God's healing work in our lives. Sadly, many of us give up on it too soon. In order to remain engaged with the healing process, you must honestly confront the question: *How healed do you want to be?*

The Big View Versus the Knothole

I have heard it said that God sees our life as if it were a parade. From His point-of-view, all of the action is visible at once as if He were gazing at it from a helicopter hovering over a parade route. From "up there" He can take in the beginning, the middle and the end of the entire parade in a single view. But He can also zoom in so as to become present to any particular part of the parade wherever and whenever He wants.

We human beings, on the other hand, do not have this divine perspective. Instead, we watch the moments and events of our lives parade by as if viewed through a knothole in a fence. Though we may try to remember what has already passed or guess at what is yet to come, most of the time our awareness is limited to the tiny bit of life within our present view. If our notion of healing is informed by God's perspective, our assumptions about it and our approach to it will be much different than our own limited perspective can provide.

One of the purposes of this book is to challenge you to see your own healing possibilities, and those of others, from God's perspective rather than through your own little knothole. Let's take a look at some ways to empower this shift in perspective:

• Embrace healing as a *process* as well as an *event* (past to present).
• Redefine healing as something that both *happens* and *continues to happen* (present to future).
• Using your eyes of faith, *envision the future age* as described by the Bible—where sickness, suffering, pain and tears will be no more (future to eternity).

This should be familiar territory for those who have become committed followers of Christ when it comes to the issue of how we view our spiritual salvation. Looking back to the cross and the resurrection of Jesus, we understand that the awesome gift of His own life has *already* addressed the issue of our sin. However, we also know that these blessings of forgiveness and salvation will only be actualized when we choose to trust Him in the *present moment*. Having trusted

Christ, we then seek to cooperate with God's saving work in an ongoing way as grace *continues* to work in us day by day. And finally, of course, we *look forward* to the salvation that awaits us at the end of the age when Christ comes again in glory.

How about You?

Are you ready to embrace a new perspective when it comes to being healed? If you have been working from an "all or nothing" approach so far, you may have become immobilized, discouraged or defeated. A new perspective on healing, however, will inspire new hope.

Where do you most profoundly feel the need for healing in your life today? Is it possible it may have already begun? Is there progress you can build on, or gains you can celebrate? I urge you to pause and reflect upon these questions. Doing so may open up new panoramas of possibility in your personal healing journey, so let the inspiration begin!

In the chapters that make up the next section of this book, we will continue to explore the possibilities that are packed into that little word *healing* by breaking it out into five distinct dimensions. Doing so will help you discern where healing may be already taking place in your life, where you need more of it, and the shape healing may take in your future. We'll begin by taking a look at the most urgent dimension of healing: *release*.

4

Release

I see my light come shinin' from the west unto to the east
Any day now, any day now,
I shall be released.

— Bob Dylan, "I Shall Be Released" (1967)

On March 30, 1981, President Ronald Reagan was ambushed by a lone assassin who lied in wait outside a Washington, D.C. hotel. Mr. Reagan was about to enter his limousine when shots were fired in his direction by a man named John Hinckley, Jr. The President was hit by one of the rounds, as were his press secretary, a secret service agent and another law enforcement authority. Thankfully, Mr. Reagan's chest wound was not fatal, and he was rushed to the hospital for treatment.

Now, I'm no doctor but I'd be willing to bet that one of the first things the surgeons wanted to do that day was get the bullet out. There would be no point in patching up the President and sending him back to the Oval Office with a foreign object still lodged in his body. There would be no point in scheduling important meetings, making TV appearances or even going home to Mrs. Reagan and his family with the bullet still doing damage to his vital systems. In other words, in order for Mr. Reagan's healing to truly begin, the bullet would have to come out—and fast.

Walking Wounded

The example of President Reagan's attempted assassination paints a vivid picture of how counter-productive it is to try to function while critically injured. But it seems to me that many people attempt living exactly this way. As they wash dishes, drive to work, study for exams, make love to their spouse, answer the telephone, pay bills or worship at church, they secretly suffer the sharp pains and debilitating consequences of an injury-producing agent lodged in their body, soul or spirit. These are the "walking wounded," and if left untreated they will become the "living dead."

A bullet doesn't care if you are a President or a pauper. It does its damage without prejudice or preference. The same is true of certain other injury-producing agents: debilitating memories of sexual abuse or other personal traumas can take root in the heart of an executive or a street bum; the burning guilt of an offended conscience can haunt a child or a grandpa; demonic spirits can influence the lives of suburban Americans or primitive animists. Young or old, black or white, male or female, powerful or cast away—the one thing the walking wounded have in common is they carry a burden that keeps them from living their best life until it is removed for good.

For this reason, the first of the five aspects of healing we will look at is the *removal of that which causes injury.* Is a woman being physically abused by her spouse? The abuse must stop for healing to begin. Is a man suffering liver damage due to his abuse of alcohol? The drinking must stop for healing to begin. Is a teenager dividing a family by acting out in angry rebellion? The acting out must cease for healing to begin. Do you see the pattern? Whether behaviors or bacteria, the things that cause injury will only continue to inflame our wounds until they are dealt with and removed.

Sometimes it seems that once an injury-producing agent is removed, healing often begins to roll out on its own. Take, for example, the way a conflicted couple can make great strides toward a more harmonious relationship by agreeing to abandon the use of any and all destructive words in their interactions. This is reflected in the Book of Proverbs where it is noted that: "Reckless words pierce like a sword, but the tongue of the wise brings healing" (12:8). If, however, one of them continues to use what I call "nuclear words," the damage to their relationship will continue no matter how many times they say "I'm sorry."

Repentance and Removal

One of the most powerful tools in healing the walking wounded is what the Bible calls *repentance*. What is biblical repentance? Put simply, it is when sinfully destructive behaviors and attitudes are first abandoned and then replaced by ones that are constructive and godly. True repentance has an emotional component of sorrow and remorse, though it is not defined by *emotions* but by *behaviors*. While feelings of regret about things we have done or left undone may move us towards repentance, these feelings are not enough. Like an unopened bud on a flower, repentance is not in full bloom until new attitudes and behaviors have replaced old ones. To repent is to purposefully remove sinful, injury-causing agents from our lives and replace them with God-given changes that bring healing, reconciliation and renewal. Quite simply, repentance begins with a sincere "I'm sorry" and is *completed* by the adoption of new actions and attitudes.

Sometimes, people confuse true biblical repentance with vague attempts to try harder. But this does not produce the kind of changes called for by true repentance. Rather than be vague, we must target specific attitudes and behaviors that offend God and bring harm to ourselves or to others. The sign of true repentance is when new life-giving, constructive and God-honoring behaviors have replaced what the Bible refers to as "dead works" (Hebrews 6:1; 9:14). Note the way in which the Apostle Paul demonstrates this in addressing how new believers in Christ should now live: "He who has been stealing must steal no longer, but must work, doing something useful with his own hands, that he may have something to share with those in need" (Ephesians 4:28). We can see here that true repentance asks more of a thief than feelings of sorrow or remorse. Instead, with God's help, Paul calls upon them to replace thieving behaviors with constructive and honest work.

When I was still a young teen, I had an opportunity to experience the difference between regret and repentance for myself. It went like this: my friends and I cooked up a scheme to go door-to-door throughout our neighborhood and sing Christmas carols. Then, before moving on, we would solicit "alms for the poor" from our audience. Before long, we had collected a significant amount of cash. And at the end of the night, we split the take between us and went home.

A couple of years later when I gave my life to Christ, a funny thing began to happen: I started to grow a conscience. From time to time I would remember things I had done—things I knew God was not pleased with—and experience a compelling need to do what I could to make things right again, if possible. One day, while passing by one of the homes we had worked during our Great Christmas Rip-off, my heart began to burn with shame and conviction. I knew I had to do something to reconcile the wrong I had done a couple of Christmas's before, but what?

Since I didn't know the people who lived there, I was at a bit of a disadvantage. But I did recall them being especially generous to us during our unholy scam. I determined to simply march up to the door, confess my deception, ask for their forgiveness and repay them my share of the loot. Every time I tried to do so, however, no one would come to the door. At first, I felt relief. Maybe God saw my sincere efforts, I reasoned, and was letting me off the hook. But in my heart I knew better. So, I decided to try a different approach.

I composed a note which I put in an envelope along with some money, and taped it to their front door one day. It read something like this:

Dear Neighbor,

A couple of Christmases ago, some friends from my street and I came to your door and sang holiday carols. You kindly invited us to come into your home and sing for your party guests as well. Afterwards, we asked you all for "alms for the poor" and you generously donated some money to us. I am ashamed to admit that we lied to you about helping the poor. We actually kept the money for ourselves. Although I cannot recall how much we collected from you at that time, I believe my portion of the proceeds came to about $20.

Recently, I became a born again follower of the Lord Jesus Christ whom I love with all my heart. I feel He wants me to confess my lie to you and give you this money as a token of my desire to make right the wrong I have done to you. Please accept this with my sincere apologies. Thank you.

To this day, I do not know what happened after I left that note. I only know that I had "produced fruit in keeping with repentance" (Matthew 3:8) and walked away feeling lighter, brighter and cleaner than before. It began when I admitted to God that I had behaved in sinful ways toward my neighbors. I know at that point, He forgave me for my sin. However, the *removal of that which had caused me injury* could not be complete until I took action to make things right with those I wronged. When I did so, I could feel the healing in my soul.

Stop Living with Toxins

Are you among the "walking wounded"? If so, healing will begin when you stop trying to live with toxic attitudes, behaviors and associations. Today is the day to make new choices—ones that move you in a God-ward direction where there is healing and light instead of shadows and decay. There, in His presence, that which has been robbing you of new life in Christ begins to lose its power. The things that have been poisoning you cannot thrive when exposed to the light of God, nor operate freely where Jesus Christ is Lord.

More and more, medical experts are discovering the invisible connections between physical diseases or dysfunctions and any number of underlying emotional, social and spiritual factors. While we can be truly grateful for the gracious gifts that come to us by means of surgical skills, medical interventions and medications, the person who wants to be "as healed as can be" will also avail themselves of Christian healing prayer, the confession of sin, and the purposeful adoption of Holy Spirit-inspired behaviors and attitudes.

Bless Your Beginnings

When it comes to our release from that which causes us injury, it is of vital importance to take a first step, no matter how feeble it may look to yourself or others. Think again of that remarkable paralyzed man who was waiting for his miracle by the Pool of Bethesda. Consider, for a moment, what it must have been like for him just after Jesus captured him in His gaze and challenged him to: "Get up! Pick up your bed, and walk!" (John 5:8). Imagine the thoughts he must have first had as he heard the voice of Jesus. He had been paralyzed for 38 years. He had no muscle tone, physical strength or sense of balance. For nearly four decades, the electrical impulses he tried to direct toward his useless legs had become lost in the malfunctioning circuitry of his nervous system leaving him flat and helpless.

Still, for some reason, something about Jesus' voice, His eyes and urgency, provoked the man to give it one more try. He pushed and there was response! He must have gasped for breath. He pushed again and his spindly legs responded. After a moment he slid his legs beneath him and pushed into a standing position for the first time in 38 years. When I think of him there, balancing in an upright position, it brings to mind the films I have seen of newborn ponies standing for the first time on their out-sized legs—a little shaky, but miraculous nonetheless.

Who knows what others thought of his first efforts that day. They may have been critical, they may have been in awe. Either way, the blockage was gone, his legs awakened and his life changed. Somehow, he stooped down, grabbed up his mat, and headed across the portico, healed! His first steps may not have been graceful, coordinated or full of precision, but every one was a miracle. That's why I want you to bless your own beginnings, whether your challenges are physical, emotional or spiritual. Your efforts may not dazzle anyone, but you can be sure that God will not despise them if they are taken by faith and empowered by grace.

There is a story I love about a mentor of mine and his oh-so-feeble attempt to take on the bitter jealousy, resentment and anger that poisoned his life during college. As he tells it, there was, in those days, a certain young lady who "hung the moon" for him and his heart belonged to her alone. However, another student came along, as he saw it, and charmed her away from him. As a result, he became filled with jealous hatred and seething resentment. Before long, he found some perverse comfort in the flame of malice that began to flicker inside of him. He welcomed its twisted energy, even if it was the energy of spite.

After awhile, his Christian friends began to notice a most unappealing change in his attitude and they came together to confront him about it. Ashamed and confused, he told them about his broken heart and the anger and jealousy he harbored within it. His friends did not hesitate to call on him to repent and release both himself and the other fellow from his bitter envy.

"You need to forgive him," they said.

"But I'm not willing to forgive him," he quickly replied.

"Then you need to pray with us that you will be willing to forgive him," they insisted.

"But I *don't want to be willing* to forgive him."

His friends would not be put off. "Then you need to pray to be willing to be willing to forgive him."

"But I *don't want to be willing to be willing* to forgive him."

"Then you need to pray to be willing, to be willing, to be willing to forgive him."

At this my friend paused. "Maybe I could do that."

And so the prayer meeting began. First, they prayed with him that the Lord would give him the grace to be willing to be willing to be willing to forgive his competitor. At some point, the injury-producing hatred began to lose its grip and he found the desire to be willing to be willing to forgive. As time went on, he found he could sincerely pray for God to make him willing to forgive. And then, finally, he tearfully asked his Lord to forgive the man whose actions had caused him such grief and pain. The bullet was out. Peace returned to his soul. Healing began.

Like the man at the Pool of Bethesda, my friend had to use whatever faith he had to do something he may at first believed to be impossible. And, as in the case of the man by the pool, the results turned out to be astonishing.

At some point following my friend's unforgettable prayer meeting, he and the young lady were reunited and, eventually, they married. Their union, now blessed by peace and generosity of spirit rather than by bitter entitlement, produced much that was good over the years that followed.

How about You?

The sources of the injuries, restrictions and dysfunctions in your life may or may not be easy to diagnose. If your obstacle to wholeness is a debilitating physical condition, a disease or a bodily injury, you may have come to accept your present condition as the way things have to be. If you are suffering the fallout of childhood abuse or abandonment, you may have come to think of yourselves as "damaged goods". If you have been lingering in the relentless pain of a betrayal, divorce, injustice or besetting fear, you may have decided that it is your lot in life or your "cross to bear" so that you have given up on looking for relief. If you have entertained habits, behaviors, attitudes and relationships that are sinful (and you know it) then you need an encounter with the One whose words can spur you on toward a miracle, just like the paralyzed man at the pool. Take a moment and listen with faith to His timeless voice. What is He saying? Stay put? Take it on the chin? Buck up? Get used to it? Tolerate it? Give in? Or, is He asking you that question of questions: "Do you want to be healed?"

The reality of the healing He offers us implies more than just the removal of the toxic things that have kept us sick, crippled, afraid or at a distance from Him. He has more, including the repair of our bodies, minds and spirits.

5

Repair

Lord, show me Your face
I'm longing for Your presence in this place
I give You all the pieces
'Cause you made a promise
You put me back together — better than I was before

— Yolanda Adams, "Show Me" (2005)

The little girl is hesitant at first. She knows His time and attention are very important. Nevertheless, her concerns push her
to seek out skills greater than her own. From what she has
heard, the man is just the sort of expert she needs.

"I hear you can heal," she says to Him.

He smiles and nods as He gently beckons her to come closer.
Reassured, she produces the patient. It is her simple doll, whose stick
leg had become detached. It would mean the world to her if He could
help make things right again. Reaching for the doll and its spindly leg,
the man carefully examines the situation. Then, skillfully, He reattach-
es it onto the doll and returns it to the happy child with a smile. All
in a day's work for the Healer from Galilee.

This sweet and imaginative scene from D.W. Griffith's silent film
classic *King of Kings* is one of my favorite movie moments. The first
time I saw it, I was delightfully surprised by the way it made me see
both healing and Jesus Christ in a new light. In only a moment's time,

it communicated compassion, care, tenderness, strength, mercy and even a little whimsy. The imagined moment shared by God's Son and a little girl takes the viewer far beyond the simple repair of a broken doll. It opens us to a greater message of love and affirmation. By tending so kindly to what mattered to her, Jesus made it clear that *she mattered* to Him.

Miracles of Repair

Of course, not all repairs are as poignant as the one in D.W. Griffith's film. Most are, in fact, rather mundane. Our cars, watches, computers, furniture, and even our bodies require skillful repair from time-to-time. Because I am not the handiest guy around, I am thankful for the people who can repair my things as needed. But to whom can we take our broken hearts, shattered dreams, dark fears, afflicted bodies or tortured memories for repair? Could it be that the bold little girl in the silent movie is giving us a message?

Griffith's fictional portrayal of Jesus and the little girl illustrates a profound biblical truth: the best place we can go with the brokenness in our lives is to God. In the pages of Scripture, we read story after story of divine intervention and repair, each encouraging us to cast "all of your cares on Him, for He cares for you" (1 Peter 5: 7). These stories stand out to us because they exceed that which is humanly possible. Most of the time, the Bible describes these miraculous repairs as taking place speedily, even instantly, after just a word, a prayer or a touch. Each act of grace serves as a signpost indicating "God was here." They interrupt our sense of normalcy, capture our attention and point us towards the One who performs wonderful works by His power.

If you find the miracles of repair that took place in Bible days inspiring, imagine how awe-inspiring it would be to witness a contemporary one. I believe that's what I was able to do in the case of Robin's brain injury

Because of the tremendous amount of head trauma she suffered in the course of the collision, Robin arrived at the hospital with several injuries to her brain. There was swelling and bleeding immediately addressed by the medical staff. But she also appeared to have suffered a certain amount of *brain shearing*. Brain shearing refers to the damage done to certain nerve fibers, called *axons*, by severe head trauma. Should these axons become overly stretched or torn, patients often experience a profound decrease in awareness, processing and function. Brain shearing is not something that self-corrects or improves with time. So, what happened to Robin?

The first hint that Robin may have experienced a miracle came during an interaction we had with several enthusiastic Intensive Care Nurses at the hospital where she recovered. Because Robin had been unconscious for the entire three weeks she had been a patient in the ICU, she wanted to return and meet her care providers and personally thank them for their care. So, we arranged for her to come for a visit one afternoon.

When the big day arrived, I rolled Robin's wheelchair through the imposing automatic doors that opened into the Intensive Care Unit, while she carefully balanced an enormous basket of candy on her lap she had prepared for the staff. As they saw her come in, several of the nurses gathered around her, full of smiles and animation. One after the other, they recounted their experiences with her as their patient while Robin did her best to take it all in.

As both Robin and I listened with fascination, the nurses reported that the first CAT scans taken of Robin after she was admitted showed evidence of brain shearing. However, on later scans, the indications were no longer there. I was intrigued by the way these seasoned nurses spoke so confidently of having witnessed a miracle. I decided I would ask Robin's neurosurgeon for more information during our next follow-up visit.

When that day arrived, I told the doctor what the nurses had reported and asked him for his opinion on the matter. Had he observed evidence of brain shearing on the earliest CAT that did not appear on later scans? He paused to consider his reply. "I thought I saw it," he said at last. I pointed out that if there had indeed been brain shearing at first, that was no longer there, then it looked to me as if a miracle had taken place. "That's your call," he responded diplomatically. "All right, then," I replied. "I'll call it a miracle!"

Whatever the scans may have shown, there is no question that

Robin's recovery was in many ways miraculous. Not only did her mental functioning return to its pre-accident level, but she took on the considerable challenge of completing a demanding accelerated Bachelors Degree program at Azusa Pacific University. As I write this, she has already begun a Masters Degree program at the same institution. Our experiences demonstrate that, not only can God repair broken lives, He can repair damaged axons too.

The Meaning of Miracles

Because they are so attention-getting, miracles remind us of God's personal involvement with the world He created. This was certainly the way Bible writers interpreted the miraculous. They understood the world and everything in it to have been made by Almighty God—the Creator existing apart from His creation so that He is neither limited by it nor dependent upon it. All of creation is an "open system" to God—one that He can affect any way He chooses. The biblical authors viewed both natural history and human events as stages upon which God chooses to make Himself known.

Sometimes God's activities are subtle and *natural*:

"*He causes His sun to rise* on the evil and the good, and *sends rain* on the righteous and the unrighteous*" (Matthew 5:45, *emphasis mine*).

At other times they are wondrously *supernatural*:

"You are *the God who performs miracles; You display Your power* among the peoples" (Psalm 77:14, *emphasis mine*).

In a way, both natural and supernatural occurrences have God's fingerprints on them. However, as we shall see, there are other forces acting upon this world and its systems.

Some of these forces are malevolent spiritual personalities described by the New Testament writers as the "rulers, authorities and powers" and "dark forces of evil". (Ephesians 6:12) Their agenda is to spread evil, destruction, harm and death into the cosmos. (Acts 10:38; John 10:10) The Bible tells us that Jesus Christ came to displace their perverse works of darkness with His acts of healing, mercy and majesty. Then, of course, the "will of man" also comes into play. (John 1:13) As these forces and their various agendas interact with one another, they produce the things we read in the newspapers, study in the classroom, and feel in the deepest part of our soul.

It is important to note that the interaction of these forces is not a showdown between equals that leaves the future up for grabs. The Bible assures us that it is God alone who possesses the ultimate authority and has the final word: "The earth is the Lord's, and everything in it, the world and all who live in it. For He has founded it upon the seas, and established it upon the waters" (Psalm 24:1, 2). Jesus asserted "all authority in heaven and on earth has been given unto Me" (Matthew 28:18).

Power Encounters

At times, the dynamic tension that exists between the will of God and the other forces at work in His world develop into what has been termed "power encounters." An outstanding biblical example of this phenomenon took place in ancient Egypt in the presence of the Great Pharaoh himself.

There, in those halls of power, Moses and the Egyptian sorcerers engaged in a spiritual showdown as the Pharaoh looked on. At first, Pharaoh's court magicians and sorcerers were able to imitate the signs and wonders performed by Moses by using the dark powers at their disposal. But there came a "boiling point" when the balance of power shifted in Moses' favor: "The magicians could not stand before Moses because of the boils; for the boil was upon the magicians, and upon all the Egyptians" (Exodus 9:11). From that point forward, the power of the Lord through Moses eclipsed the inferior sorceries of the Pharaoh's magicians.

This power encounter clearly demonstrated that Moses' miracle-working power came from a different source than that of the Egyptian conjurers. He had come in the Name of "I Am" (Exodus 3:14) and was, therefore, expressing the power of the True and Living God. By doing so, Moses bore witness to the supremacy of his God. He also added impact to his demands that Pharaoh "let My people go." When both human will and demonic powers eventually submitted to Moses' God-given authority, the Exodus was born.

The Bible teaches that God not only exercises His power and

authority over living things and conscious powers, but also over the organic, atomic, interstellar and sub-atomic dimensions of the natural world. So, biblical miracles involve not only the transformation of people and human events, but also such phenomena as "signs and wonders" in nature, the multiplication of food, the stilling of tumultuous sea storms and the molecular transformation of water into wine. There are biblical miracles of provision, rescue and even a specific and miraculous display of God's radiant glory in the earthly body of Jesus Christ. (See Daniel 6:27; Acts 4:30; Mark 9:2; Matthew 14:21, John 2:11; Exodus 15:4; Acts 27:23, 24)

When comparing the portrayal of miracles in the Old Testament versus the New Testament, Bible readers notice a startling difference. The abundance of powerful miracles that come with the earthly ministry of Jesus Christ and His apostles hint that the heavenly floodgates have opened at last. It is as if the great heart of God, overflowing with divine love, has finally released on the desperately needy world He came to save. The result is a spiritual outpouring that continues to drench the Earth to this day—an outpouring of divine power and mercy in Jesus' Name.

Behind the Miracles

Most biblical miracles of healing are described as bodily repairs, or in terms of the removal, or expulsion, of demonic spirits. These acts of removal or repair as performed by Christ and His apostles take place in a variety of settings, both public and private. Those who witnessed them were amazed at what they saw. Sometimes, the healings were so prolific that, rather than describe them each one, Bible writers summarized them en masse.

Healing miracles in the Bible include such "repairs" as:

• Reversals of paralysis (Matthew 9:1-8)
• Recovery of sight and voice after a demon is cast out (Matthew 12:22)
• Recovery of sight by the blind (Matthew 9:27)
• The removal of leprosy and miraculous repair of the flesh (Luke 5:12–19)

- The repair of continuous feminine bleeding (Matthew 9: 20–22)
- The repair of swollen tissue from an unspecified cause ("dropsy" in Luke 14:1-6)
- The repair of a "withered" hand (Luke 6:6–11)
- The repair of a crippled man's condition by the Apostle Paul (Acts 14:10)
- The repair of a crippled man's condition by Peter and John (Acts 3:6-9)

The list goes on. It is important, then, to be aware of how often the Bible speaks of healing in terms of miraculous repair. Why? Because of the way it influences our own notions of what healing is all about. In the Bible, we read again and again of diseases, sicknesses and injuries that are instantaneously repaired by divine power and authority. While this is undoubtedly inspiring, it also makes it easy for us to assume that healing only comes in one package: miraculous bodily repair. If, however, we look closely and thoughtfully at the biblical texts, we will discover that there is more.

While a great many of biblical healings involve the reversal of physical symptoms, we see evidence of psychological, spiritual and relational repair as well. Take, for example, the case of the uncontrollable demonized man from the region of the Gaderenes in Mark, chapter five. Due to his outbursts of violence, this poor, tormented soul was doomed to spend his days in isolation and neglect, living among the tombs. It was there, in this unlikely setting, that a power encounter developed between the cruel demons living in this man and the Lord Jesus Christ who set him free.

Afterwards, the stunned locals were shocked to find this once hopeless case "sitting, and clothed, and in his right mind" (Mark 5: 15). It would be difficult to find a more dramatic instance of the repair of a man's shattered social and psychological state in any case study, modern or ancient.

Still Happening Today?

I believe God still does miracles of healing in the name of Jesus Christ. Sometimes they take place rapidly—even instantly—while, on other occasions, they occur over time. Fast or slow, large or small, miracles of healing and repair continue to bear witness to the goodness and the greatness of God. That's why I want to conclude this chapter by telling you about one of the most remarkable instances of a "time-released" miracle that I have ever seen. It happened, and is still happening; to a friend I'll call Janice.

When I first met Janice, she stood out from the others who regularly attended our church's adult singles fellowship. Her appearance, her manner and her personal presentation telegraphed the message that she was having a hard time managing even the basics of life. As we got to know her, we learned that Janice had been diagnosed with "Dissociative Identity Disorder" (or DID). Her condition (formerly known as "multiple-personality disorder") typically stems from extreme childhood trauma and abuse. In order to survive the unimaginable horrors of a tortured childhood, Janice's core personality had "split" into a number of identities, each having their own distinctive characteristics. There was no doubt that Janice was a true believer in Jesus Christ, but it was hard for her to trust anyone consistently, including God.

Despite these considerable social obstacles, Janice seemed to find a place of acceptance, love and safety in our singles group and she kept returning. As we came to know her better, we learned that she was a very intelligent and capable person who could play a musical instrument well and had other considerable abilities. She was under professional psychological care, but her low-income status meant that it was somewhat inconsistent. As she grew to trust us and our approach to healing ministry, she started to receive personal prayer from several people on a regular basis. Most of the time, her reaction to these ministry experiences were fairly low-key: appreciative, but not necessarily dramatic. Nevertheless, Janice continued to accept whatever help we could offer her.

For a long time, it seemed as if Janice borrowed some of our faith in God to supplement her own. She was clear about the basics of the Gospel message and had an intellectual grasp of the fatherhood of God. But the abuse she suffered from her earthly father made it difficult for her to make an emotional connection with her Heavenly

Father—that He loved her and wanted good things for her. Still, Janice kept showing up for more fellowship, more personal ministry and more belonging. Little by little, a miracle of transformation began to take shape.

Years later, Janice is still in my life. She is so fundamentally different from the person I have just described that it has taken me considerable effort to recall her former way of living. Repaired by grace, she has come to see God, other people and herself in radically different terms than she used to. I still chuckle when I think of the Sunday several years ago when she approached me after church to boast that she was now wearing matching socks two days per week! Today, Janice not only matches her socks each day, she has learned how to dress quite smartly on a limited budget. There are many people I know who would love to have such a practical skill!

Janice would tell you her biggest healing breakthrough came with the repair of her image of God. It began when she finally grasped that He does not hate her (a stubborn lie that once ruled her life). As time passed, she went on to accept that He, in fact, truly loves her! In addition, I have enjoyed witnessing the repair of her once-fragmented soul. Even the various personalities that arose from the extreme childhood trauma she suffered have successfully re-integrated back into her core personality. It has been a wonder to behold.

Today Janice holds a regular job and has become self-sufficient. Best of all, the healing she has undergone has given her something valuable to share with others. Her unique ability to offer hope stems from the ways that God's saving, healing, transforming love and power have impacted her over years of time.

Never Give Up

I'm quite sure that Janice would not credit one single experience of prayer, counseling, intervention, encouragement, exhortation, socialization or medication for her miraculous transformation. Rather, all of these things have played a role in helping her toward wholeness and new life. If there is a secret to Janice's miracle it is simply that she never gave up. Whatever embarrassment, confusion, thresholds of trust, or discouraging setbacks she ran into, she always managed to find a way to keep moving forward. This persevering grace enabled her to consolidate the gains she made until they became evident to all.

How about You?

Maybe you find yourself in need of a miracle repair. Like the little girl with the broken doll, you may be looking for someone you can trust who is strong enough, wise enough and kind enough to fix what is broken around you and inside of you. I urge you to imitate her example and draw close to Jesus. As you present your specific needs to Him, you can be sure He will care for you and welcome your requests for help. If your faith is weak, I urge you to learn from Janice and call upon others who can share their stronger faith with you. Pulling God and others closer to us when we need help the most can change our "mourning into dancing" (Psalm 30:11).

6

Restore

I waited patiently for the Lord
He inclined and heard my cry
He brought me up out of the pit
Out of the miry clay

I will sing, sing a new song
I will sing, sing a new song

— U2, "Forty"

It had been several months since the accident and Robin was back home again, but life was far from normal. Because of her many broken bones, she was forced to spend most of her day and every night downstairs in a rented hospital bed. Each night, I would kiss her before climbing the stairs to our room to sleep alone. It was quiet in the house, except for the slight hissing noise that came from the baby monitor on the night stand next to me. That tiny speaker kept me connected to her through those long nights when she might need me and call out my name. The hardest part was to hear her groan in pain every so often as I lay in bed staring into space, unable to help. Sometimes I would go downstairs anyway, slipping through the silence to quietly pray for her, gently stroke her forehead or just tuck her in one more time.

Thank God, Robin was home at last. But the road to recovery would still be long and difficult. There would be more surgeries, hours of physical therapy and at least a hundred other obstacles to confront. She lost nearly everything but her life on that rainy day in February several years before, including her identity, lifestyle, sense of well-being—even her spiritual spark. Mixed together with steel, blood and steam, the life she once knew had somehow become a part of the roadside wreckage the ambulance left behind.

Robin was still a mom, but there was little she could do for her children. She could not help them with their homework or cheer for them at their games. She could not tuck them in to bed or read a story before switching off the light. She was still a wife, but there was not much she could do for me—make a nice meal, share the details of my day or hold me in her arms before sleeping. And she was still a nurse, but she could not report for duty. She could no longer help first-time mothers with their newborn children or assist doctors during surgery. These days, Robin's trips to the hospital were as a patient, not a caregiver. It was a role she neither wanted nor enjoyed.

Thankfully, with time, grace and hard work, progress came. As the months passed and her body began to mend, the dim outline of a real future reappearing day by day. Like tiles in a mosaic, the pieces of Robin's shattered life began to come together again and we marked and celebrated each milestone. Some of these were the big triumphs, such as regaining her ability to drive again. Others appeared quietly, almost imperceptibly, but as they grew in number they stoked the fires of hope..

Perhaps the day I'll remember best from that period is the one Robin and her physical therapist attempted to climb all the way up the stairs to the second story of our house. It wasn't easy, but their efforts paid off. As Robin stood on the upper landing and looked through the door into her own bedroom, she wept. It must have seemed like a dream to her. She hadn't seen it for seven months.

About a year following her release from the hospital, we bought a home on the other side of the community and moved in. This new house symbolized a fresh start for our family. By the grace of God our young church plant was thriving. We could see other signs that our lives were moving forward, too. In the spring, our two older sons graduated—one from high school and the other from college. Attending their commencement ceremonies together was a joy for us. Day by day, Robin regained her strength and became more active again. We found ourselves giving thanks for even the smallest of mercies, as if we were learning how to count our blessings for the first time.

The Big Question

In spite of all the progress and blessings, a stubborn question haunted us—especially Robin. It was a question that physical progress or the recovery of our normal way of life could not erase. It was the question of "Why?" Why had God allowed the crash? Why did it have to happen at a time when we were just beginning a new mission for Him? Why was she so brutally injured? Where was God's protection when we needed it most?

At that time, Robin had to face those "why" questions daily. Each one that passed was filled with a variety of issues related to her recovery, pain management and her overall restoration. Sometimes, late at night, we would lie in bed and talk about what had happened, wondering why God had allowed it. Yes, we were thankful she had not been killed. Yes, we were grateful to be together again. Yes, we were in awe of how well our children came through the trial that was redirecting the trajectory of our family history. We praised God for the new home, the kind friends and the other resources He had blessed us with in the midst of it all. But Robin felt stuck. She needed resolution, some sense of rhyme or reason. Without those things, there were days she wondered if she could go on living at all.

I tried to listen and understand—her pain, her doubts and her conflicts—but I knew I could not possibly provide the answers for which she was looking. How could I speak for the Almighty? Who was I to be His apologist? Rather than try to provide answers, I told her of my growing conviction that, on this side of eternity, we may have to live without them: "For who has known the mind of the Lord, that he may instruct Him?" (I Corinthians 2:16a).

There was only one thing I felt I could offer, the thing most responsible for keeping me sane in the midst of our life-shaking crisis. It was the simple, undeniable conviction that God had *been present with us* through it all. Looking back, I could see how God was at the accident scene itself. I could see how He was there with her throughout her long stay at the hospital. I could even see how He remained present to us while we struggled with our doubts and fears. This knowledge that God was there had somehow become enough for me and I hoped it could be enough for her, too.

Surprising Principles

It was through this dark and difficult period that we came to learn a rather unexpected truth about restoration. We discovered, to our surprise, that we did not need to have "all the answers" for restoration to occur. As we stumbled through our doubts and questions, we found that it was *the presence of God* that gave us the strength to go on, not a pocketful of answers.

The harsh realities that sometimes rattle our sense of connection with God are not, in themselves, strong enough to truly shut Him out. Through the years, I have learned the paths that lead us through life's dark valleys cannot separate us from His love. Even brick walls of doubt cannot hold Him back. The Bible assures us "if we are faithless, He will remain faithful, for he cannot disown Himself" (2 Timothy 2:13). We can trust that even if our grip on Him may seem weak, He will never let go of us. Like the wind, rain, or warm sunshine, *the presence of God can find its way through even the smallest crack* in the wall of our doubts and fears and reach us in those places where we wait for Him alone.

There is nothing wrong with our inability to provide easy answers to life's perplexing questions. Turn through the pages of history and you'll see it is simply human. A careful review of the lives of our Bible heroes reveals that they were ordinary men and women who distinguished themselves by daring to trust God beyond the point where life made any sense. These courageous souls "... faced jeers and flogging, while still others were chained and put in prison. They were stoned; they were sawed in two; they were put to death by the sword. They went about in sheepskins and goatskins, destitute, persecuted and mistreated—the world was not worthy of them. They wandered in deserts and mountains, in caves and in holes in the ground. These were all commended for their faith..." (Hebrews 11:36–39a).

A Mission That Heals

As Robin emerged from her dark night of the soul, she began to feel a strong desire to share her story with others. Nearly two years after the crash, her first opportunity to do so arrived. The occasion was a Ladies' Holiday Tea event that our new church was putting on before Christmas. Robin was invited to give the keynote talk. Right away, she knew she wanted to invite some of the people who had witnessed various portions of her recovery process to share the stage with her.

When the day of the Tea arrived, the beautifully-appointed room was full of women who had come to hear Robin speak and enjoy the seasonal atmosphere. As the speaking part of the program got underway, some of Robin's invited guests spoke of how they had been inspired by her miraculous rebound.

When it came to Robin's turn to take the podium, she told the women the tragic details of her story. The people in her audience were quite obviously moved. It was clear to everyone that the woman standing before them was a miracle. As she finished her talk, the ladies present responded with an enthusiastic display of support, love and appreciation.

This first opportunity was followed by others. Each time, Robin learned another lesson about the blessings that come when you freely give yourself to others. Sharing her inspiring story provided a unique way to experience her own progress and restoration. Was God actually turning Robin's difficulties and losses into a source of blessing and encouragement for herself and others? It seemed He was.

You Want to Do What?

One day Robin approached me with an extra-special inspiration. If possible, she would find every fireman, paramedic and highway patrolman at the scene of her accident and personally thank them. This would be no small task; the list of first-responders totaled 27!

But I was learning that these inspired missions helped Robin reclaim her life from the chaos that had nearly extinguished it.

First, she recruited a photographer friend to take an up-to-date photo of her and our two "accident kids". Then the photos were duplicated, framed and prepared for distribution. Below the photographic image were the words:

Because You Made a Difference. February 10, 2000.
With Gratitude from Robin, Andrew and Jeanne Ann Faris

She then hired a local chocolatier to make statuettes resembling those presented each year at the Academy Awards in Hollywood. Each chocolate Oscar was covered in gold foil and combined with a framed photo to make up a gift package—her way of honoring each person's performance on the scene.

Robin enlisted the help of firefighter friends of our family to assist in tracking down the individuals who had come to her aid. Once she knew where to find them, Robin visited the various firehouses where they were stationed and presented her thank-you packages to them. She did the same for the two highway patrol officers who had come. The responses she received amazed her. Many of the men noted that it was rare for anyone to come back and say "thank you."

Another Lesson

To our surprise, these experiences highlighted one of God's key restoration principles: "Give and it will be given unto you. A good measure, pressed down, shaken together and running over, will be poured into your lap. For with the measure you use, it will be measured to you" (Luke 6:38). Clearly it was God who had inspired Robin to show her gratitude, share her testimony, and thank her doctors, first-responders, physical therapists, family, friends and others. As a result of her willingness to share her story and the genuine thankfulness in her heart, Robin's own healing and restoration were multiplied. In other words, the best thing she could do for herself was *focus on others.*

Major holidays provided the perfect opportunity for Robin to go back to the Intensive Care Unit and the Recovery Unit of the hospital with a huge gift basket of seasonal candy for the nurses and other caregivers. Of course, they were delighted to see her (and the candy!) and they marveled again and again in her recovery. Her photo had even found a place of honor on the ICU "Wall of Fame" where patient success stories were celebrated. These visits gave everyone a chance to feel like a winner each time they occurred.

Before long, Robin was receiving invitations to share her story at church retreats, hospital fundraising dinners and other events. One evening, I stood proudly her as she addressed the annual promotions ceremony for the Orange County Fire Authority. But it did not stop there for Robin: she loved sharing her story with anyone interested to hear it. She was on fire!

What is Restoration?

Robin's story powerfully illustrates God's power to restore our lives in the aftermath of brokenness, injury, spiritual crisis and personal distress. It's important to build some framework around our study of the word *restoration*, which I define as *the recovery of that which has been lost, stolen or otherwise taken away.*

The Bible portrays God's restoration work on both a grand, cosmic scale and on a personal level. On the macro level, the Bible teaches that the world was once more perfect than it is now. When sin (the open rejection of God's will) entered the world through the first human beings, it opened the door to injustice, oppression, immorality, sickness, disease, war, division, abuse and every kind of evil. This is why we speak of the present world as fallen. Only God can lift it again.

This plunge from perfect innocence was comprehensive in that it affects the spiritual, the social and the environmental dimensions of creation. What began as "very good" in God's estimation (Genesis 1:31) fell into bondage because of sin (Romans 8:21). Not only did sin pollute the first human parents, it also spread to every one of their offspring—including you and me! As a result, we each carry within ourselves a nagging sense of paradise lost. Much of our life is spent trying to regain paradise through how we work, whom we love, and what we know. Our quest for restoration comes to us naturally.

The Bible makes it clear; however, that paradise cannot be regained by our own efforts. We need God to make things right again. That is why its pages chart the story of the greatest restoration plan the world will ever see—a plan that finds its ultimate expression in the death and resurrection of God's Son, Jesus Christ: "You see, at just the right time, when we were still powerless, Christ died for the ungodly. Very rarely will anyone die for a righteous man, though for a good man someone might possibly dare to die. But God demonstrates His own love for us in this: While we were still sinners, Christ died for us" (Romans 5:6–8).

The salvation God invites us to experience through Christ is just one aspect of the coming restoration of all things, which He will bring to pass at the end of the age. In the meantime, acts of inspired kindness, mercy and service reveal the manifested, or "dancing hand," of God in this broken world as He touches it with His restoring love.

The resulting social lift produced by this influx of grace can be tracked statistically in the aftermath of a great revival or people movement toward Christ. Often, there is a discernable dip in crime, an increase in prosperity and new social stability that occurs when large numbers of people turn to Jesus. The reduction in disorderly conduct, social dysfunctions and family disintegration produces benefits across the board as various societal diseases and injustices begin to loosen their grip. What begins as a spiritual restoration spreads into many other dimensions of life like concentric circles in a pond.

Ultimate restoration—as foreseen in the resurrection of Jesus—is already at work in those who believe in the form of an unquenchable divine power (Ephesians 2:1–10; 1 John 5:11–13). We are saved "not because of the righteous things we have done," writes the Apostle Paul, "but because of His mercy... through the washing of rebirth and renewal of the Holy Spirit whom He poured out on us generously through Jesus Christ our Savior" (Titus 3:5,6). The ultimate outworking of this already-initiated plan of salvation will include the remaking and restoration of the very cosmos itself: "And He that sat upon the throne said, 'Behold, I make all things new.' And He said unto me: 'Write; for these words are true and faithful'" (Revelation 21:5).

The Restoration Ministry of Jesus

Healing ministry, such as we see in the life of Jesus and His apostles, provides another avenue for the expression of God's restoration power. When Jesus healed the man with a withered hand, Luke describes the transformation as an act of restoration. His healed hand is said to have been "restored whole as the other" (Luke 6:10). These micro-restorations are hints of a coming mega-restoration. At that time, the entire created order will be transformed by God following the great judgments He will make, and following the return of Jesus Christ and His reign upon this earth.

In addition to the outward physical acts of restoration we see in Jesus' healing ministry, the Bible also gives us examples of profound interior changes inspired by Christ. A delightful example of such change is found in the gospel account of a tax-collector named Zacchaeus.

Zacchaeus was wealthy, but it seemed that much of his riches were gained by dishonest means. Specifically, he had been abusing his authority as a hired tax collector for the Romans, cheating his own people out of their hard-earned cash.

One evening, a most unlikely set of circumstances brought Jesus to the home of Zacchaeus. That night, Zacchaeus underwent a most remarkable inner transformation. It became obvious when, during dinner, a "new" Zacchaeus stood up to make an announcement: "Look, Lord!, here and now I give half of my possessions to the poor, and if I have cheated anybody out of anything, I will pay back four times the amount" (Luke 19:8). Once again, spiritual transformation found expression in very practical matters. This pleased Jesus who affirmed Zacchaeus's newfound generosity by declaring: "Today salvation has come to this house, because this man, too, is a son of Abraham. For the Son of Man came to seek and to save what was lost" (Luke 19:9,10).

Because there are so many different kinds of losses, reversals, injustices and brokenness in the world, we should not be surprised to find restoration taking place in a wide variety of ways. Social destruction, war, corruption and injustice have rolled like mighty waves of destruction through human history, wreaking every kind of havoc.

Yet, God promises that a day will come when these things will cease forever and be set right. At that time, "He will wipe every tear from their eyes. There will be no more death or mourning or crying or pain, for the old order of things has passed away" (Revelation 21:4).

How about You?

What is it in your life or in your environment that is awaiting restoration? Is it your bodily health? Your spiritual life? Your emotional well-being? Your personal relationships? Have you undergone a period of loss, reversal, brokenness or grief that has left you feeling stripped and diminished—as if something has been taken away from you? If so, I urge you to pursue true spiritual restoration by seeking Jesus Christ with intensity. In seeking more of God in your life, you will lay the foundation for all other kinds of restoration to take place.

I also pray that you have been inspired by the remarkable lessons Robin learned in the course of her recovery and restoration. Do you recall the way her commitment to give what she could to others invited blessings back into her own life? What do you have—large or small—to share with others? How might sharing your life, trials and victories energize your own restoration process?

Some of the primary ways to increase a felt sense of God's presence in our lives includes worship, prayer, healing ministry, Bible reading and fellowship with other believers. Even if you don't have answers to all the "whys" of the challenges you face, God's presence can comfort, strengthen and empower you. By drawing near to the One who restores, you can experience your own redemption and lift!

Robin and I learned that good things happen when we turn our wounds into wellsprings and our messes into messages. Tragedies, losses and failures can take us to the edge of the danger zone, but the trip back very often puts us into God's great story of redemption where, as one Keith Green put it, "trials turn to gold."

7

Redeem

I believe in miracles
I believe in dreams
Through the pain I've come to know
How far the heart can reach
A spark of hope
In sorrows place
Will shine
With such amazing grace
Stronger than before"
— Olivia Newton John, Annie Roboff, Beth Nielsen Chapman,
"Stronger Than Before" (2005)

But I have prayed for you, Simon, that your faith may not fail.
And when you have turned back, strengthen your brothers"
— Luke 22:32

Bethany Hamilton was 13 years old when she lost her left arm during a Tiger shark attack off the North Shore of Kaui, Hawaii. At that time, Bethany was already becoming known in the world of amateur surf competition as a true up-and-comer. The road (or shall we say wave) ahead looked golden for the young woman whose parents, Tom and Cheri Hamilton, had her on surfboards from the time she could walk. But on Halloween Day 2003, the attack Bethany endured from an aggressive 14-foot shark threatened to crush her dreams forever.

After multiple surgeries, the young surfer successfully recovered from the physical damage of the attack. Next, she would have to face the question of whether she would, or even could, surf again. Less than a month after her ordeal, Bethany was back in the water. She was determined to develop a new technique for herself that would allow her to compete in the surfing world again. It wouldn't be easy, but Bethany was determined to get back in the game.

Throughout her childhood, the young surfer had nurtured a strong personal faith in Jesus Christ. Her maturing faith inspired Bethany to treat the shark attack as something God allowed her to go through—something that could be turned for His glory. Of course, news of her attack placed her in the worldwide media spotlight. But somehow Bethany seemed ready.

As her story became known, her indomitable spirit and positive "can do" attitude began to inspire people everywhere. "I don't pretend to have all the answers to why bad things happen to good people," she later wrote. "But I do know that God knows all those answers, and sometimes He lets you know in this life, and sometimes He asks you to wait so that you can have a face-to-face talk about it." Such characteristic honesty endeared Bethany to a host of people around the world who had become aware of her challenges. Could a young person like her really make a comeback from such devastating circumstances?

As it turned out, Bethany's comeback was stunning. After only a few months, she began to win and place in prestigious surfing competitions in spite of her lack of a left arm. Over the next several years her amazing accomplishments and personal testimony opened doors for her to communicate her story to millions of people. Along with newspapers and magazines, Bethany's story was also being featured on television news segments and talk shows. "I guess they see me as a symbol of courage and inspiration," she said. "One thing hasn't changed—and that's how I feel when I'm riding a wave. It's like, here I am. I'm still here. It's still me and my board in God's ocean."

Ever since the attack first took place, Bethany has continued to turn her tragedy into a triumph. She was appointed chairwoman of Beating the Odds Foundation and has served as a spokesperson for the international compassion ministry of World Vision. Her autobiography, Soul Surfer, was published as well as Christian devotional books for teens. A film version of Bethany's story is also in the works. Speaking of his daughter's outstanding example of faith, Tom Hamilton observes: "Somehow God gave Bethany an amazing amount of grace in this. I am in awe. She never asks, "Why me?"' For Bethany, the "whys and wherefores" are simple: "This was God's plan for my life and I'm going to go with it."

Messes into Messages

Bethany Hamilton's story is a great illustration of *redemption*; the fourth component of our five-dimensional healing model. What is redemption? One dictionary defines the word "redeem" as "to buy back, repurchase, to get or win back".[1] This could mean many things. For example, while Bethany will never get her arm back, her hopes, dreams and vision for living have returned—and then some! In the long run, her losses have been mightily redeemed for higher purposes than competitive success. They have provided Bethany with a way to bear witness to Christ and inspire others, having been "bought back" from disaster to bring blessing instead of despair. This phenomenon is not new. God has a long history of turning our messes into messages, our trials into triumphs and our tests into testimonies! How does He do this? By the power of something the Bible calls grace.

Holy Electricity

What is grace? Put simply, it is God's active power at work in us. Grace begins with God and then it moves out to catch us in its power. Once grace has grabbed us, it draws us toward God. In this way we are lifted to new heights through a power not our own. The net result is that God gets glory through lives like ours and we experience salvation and wholeness as God's unmerited favor works in us: "For it is by grace you have been saved—through faith, and this is from yourselves, it is the gift of God" (Ephesians 2:8).

Grace is made up of both a passive and an active component. The passive component is mercy. Mercy makes it possible for God to justly spare us from the judgment we deserve for our sins and offenses so that they are *passed over*. The active component of grace is *power*. The activated power of grace goes to work within us, bringing about real changes in what we believe, how we act and how we live. I like to think of it as holy electricity; once we are plugged into the supercharged current of God's amazing grace, anything can happen!

But how do we "plug in" to grace? The Bible tells us how: by putting our faith in Jesus Christ. "Therefore, since we have been justified through faith, we have peace with God through our Lord Jesus Christ, through whom we have gained access by faith into this grace in which we now stand" (Romans 5:1–2a). By trusting in Christ, God's saving and healing grace is released into our lives. The Apostle Paul credits this active dimension of grace for the changes in his life when he writes: "But by the grace of God I am what I am, and his grace to me was not without effect. No, I worked harder than all of them—yet not I, but the grace of God that was with me" (1 Corinthians 15:10).

Unlike the various change agents and powers we find in the natural world, grace is neither random nor impersonal. God's grace works in us according to His plans and purposes—with the ultimate goal of making us like His Son, Jesus Christ. This has always been God's endgame since everything good, worthy and lasting finds its ultimate expression in Christ. The Bible tells us that He, Jesus, holds the unique place of being the eternal beloved of God, the Father. To be included by grace into this love affair is life-changing, indeed!

Sometimes we try to bring about change in our lives by means other than grace. We may be tempted to turn to guilt, especially religious and social guilt, rather than grace in our ongoing quest for change. In fact, guilt "works" in that it can drive us toward certain kinds of change (at least for awhile). Guilt is plenteous, often potent, and always within our reach. Guilt, I often joke with friends, is the gift that keeps on giving. Yet, guilt-driven change lacks the purity, longevity or redemptive quality produced by grace-activated change. Dr. Henry Cloud humorously illustrates this in his book *How People*

Grow when he summarizes some of the sermons he has heard as follows:

1. God is good.
2. You're not.
3. Try harder.[2]

While it can succeed in making us aware of our deficits, guilt is powerless to "buy them back" or effectively turn them for good. It is not, in a word, redemptive. Thankfully, where guilt falls short, grace excels! While guilt can only take us as far as despair and regret, grace leads us all the way to God via true repentance and surrender. There, before the Lord Himself, we discover the real power point of redemption and transformation: actual fellowship with God!   And that's where real healing begins.

Popular commentator and blogger, La Shawn Barber, tells the story of how she discovered this critical difference between self-generated change and the redemptive power of God's grace. Since the time she was a teenager, La Shawn had become daily dependent on alcohol. She had also become sexually promiscuous. It wasn't until she was nearly 30 that she decided the time had come to change her life. Rather than turn to established recovery groups like AA, La Shawn vowed to break her addictions without outside help. Looking back, she sees now that her motives were deeply rooted in self-sufficiency and pride: "I thought if I could stop cold turkey, without help from anyone, I would get all the recognition," she wrote. After awhile, however, her "white knuckle" approach to personal transformation proved to be far less than fulfilling:

> Two years into my sobriety and sexual abstinence ... I was no longer promiscuous, nor was I drinking; but something was missing. I still thirsted for the drink. I still craved the touch of a man's hands on my body. Two years of abstinence didn't seem so vast an accomplishment anymore.
>
> My lifelong tendency to isolate myself continued into my sobriety. Instead of sitting alone in my apartment drinking beer and imagining drinking myself to death, I'd sit alone in my

apartment sipping herbal tea, reading and obsessing about my life. I wasn't growing in any way, especially spiritually. I was a 'dry drunk,' a term used by alcoholics to describe someone who no longer drinks but who still thinks and acts like an alcoholic.[3]

La Shawn's healing was only partially complete. While her new way of living was an improvement over her addictive lifestyle, she found it to be surprisingly hollow and unsatisfying. At that point, she had yet to understand the new life she had been looking for was not merely a matter of successful abstinence. To find it she would need a total spiritual healing—and that would only come through a total surrender of herself to God. Thanks in part to the prayers and influence of her vibrantly Christian sister, La Shawn's day of grace arrived at last. The difference it made was both profound and ongoing:

> As I read the Bible, I began to understand that I hadn't stopped drinking under my own power. But for God's goodness, I'd still be a drunk or worse. It was all God's work, and He was ready for me whether or not I was ready for Him. He'd sustained me through the long months of sobriety and turned me away from fleshly pursuits. He got the credit, not I.
>
> Through the years, He's shown me that what I thought was my own work was actually His way of drawing me to Him. It is through Jesus Christ I am made right with God. By His goodness alone, I have been forgiven. He took the despair of drinking myself into oblivion and turning to men for physical gratification and shaped it into a love for the Bible and a desire to share it with others.[4]

The Mystery of Redemption

Can God really take bad things and turn them for good? This is one of the great mysteries of the Christian Faith, and yet there is no doubt that the answer is a resounding "yes!" No one, for example, would describe the brutal arrest, conviction, punishment and crucifixion of an innocent man as a "good" thing. And yet, God turned the pain and suffering of His beloved Son into the single greatest means of grace the world will ever know. That's the power of God's redeeming grace.

We have hints of this paradox in the natural world, such as when garbage is turned into fuel by a man-made process known as "biomass gasification".[5] One such system features elaborately designed plants that turn mountains of waste into clean, green electric power.

Now, if human beings can turn garbage into fuel, imagine what God can do with our errors, mistakes, tragedies, deficiencies and sins. How He redeems these things for good is something of a mystery—one that lies at the heart of the message of the New Testament. And yet, one of the great features of the Gospel of Jesus Christ is the way it boldly proclaims that God is bigger than the things we do or those that are done to us. In the end, it is God who gets the last word about how our lives will turn out if we will humble ourselves and put our entire being into His hands. We see this splendidly displayed in the life of the Apostle Paul. In his day, this former enemy of Christ became one of God's trophies—a man whose transformed life put God's redeeming power on display.

Before surrendering his life to Christ, Paul spent all his energy on the pursuit of a righteous life as defined by a particular brand of Jewish religious discipline. His redemption story, like La Shawn Barber's, begins as a story of his own will power and accomplishments: "A Hebrew of Hebrews, in regard to the law, a Pharisee; as for zeal, persecuting the church, as for legalistic righteousness, faultless!" (Philippians 3:5-6). The time would come, however, when he would see his self-generated goodness as entirely without value, considering it all loss for the sake of Christ. In essence, his self-exalting life had reached a dead end. If he could not achieve religious perfection through his very best efforts, he had nowhere left to go. But none of Paul's misguided efforts, or even his sinful errors, could hold back the redeeming hand of the One who loved him.

Paul, who considered himself "the worst of sinners" (1 Timothy 3:1), was a perfect candidate to put God's mercy and power on display. The fact that he had gotten things so very wrong in his pre-conversion life would only amplify the majesty and glory of the One who had repurchased him for a greater purpose. "Yes, I was the worst of sinners," he admits. "But for that very reason I was shown mercy so that in me, the worst of sinners, Christ Jesus might display his unlimited patience as an example for those who would believe on him and receive eternal life" (1 Timothy 1:14-16).

The memory of his past life, though in many ways lamentable, did not lock Paul into a place of despair. Instead, he came to see his exceptional blindness and error as an opportunity for God to tell His saving story. "Imagine that," Paul says in effect, "God has mysteriously turned my obvious defects into a spiritually-potent advertisement for grace!"

If it sounds like I'm praising sin, I'm not. Sin is never celebrated in the Bible. But the Apostle Paul repeatedly expresses his awe at the way grace never allows sin to get the last word in the lives of His redeemed. In fact, he points out that the harder sin tries, the more grace succeeds: "What shall we say, then? Shall we go on sinning that grace may increase?" His answer is clear and quick: "By no means! We died to sin; how can we live in it any longer?" (Romans 6:1-2). Redemption is not our story to write by willfully continuing in sin. It is God's story to write by turning our sin, faults and tragedies into an opportunity for His excellent grace to be displayed.

How about You?

What is your attitude toward your reversals, deficits, flaws and sins? Does it feel to you as if they have become the things that most define you? Has their presence in your life convinced you that you are beyond hope—too far gone to be good for anything or anyone? Do you wish you were someone else with more to offer God or fewer obstacles to overcome? Have your physical illnesses, bodily deficits, emotional struggles or personal problems threatened to disqualify you from being used by God or living a victorious life? Then hear afresh the voice of your Redeemer as He declares His mercy and grace to you through the words He spoke to His wandering people of old:

> I will repay you for the years the locusts have eaten—
>   the great locust and the young locust,
>   the other locusts and the locust swarm —

My great army that I sent among you.
You will have plenty to eat, until you are full,
and you will praise the name of the LORD your God,
who has worked wonders for you;
never again will my people be shamed.
Then you will know that I am in Israel,
that I am the LORD your God,
and that there is no other;
never again will my people be shamed

— Joel 2:25-27

Even now, the "divine electricity" of saving grace is at work in your body, soul, mind, spirit and personal history. Mysteriously, God is working out His master plan to make you more like Christ. In His own way He is telling His story through your story—warts, faults, impairments and all! He has no *perfect* people through whom He can display His splendor. Instead, He just uses people *perfectly*. Could there be anything better than knowing there is nothing that exists, nothing you have done and nothing that has been done to you that lies beyond the redeeming grasp of grace? To know and experience this mystery is to know what it means to be healed.

God is in the "buy back" business. There are no wasted tears, dreams or prayers in His kingdom. The greatest gift you have to give to others may very well proceed out of your deepest wound, greatest struggle or largest deficit. Someone has said that it is the wounded bird that sings the sweetest song.

And yet, there is another dimension of healing beyond the discovery of God's redeeming power. It is perhaps the least understood and rarest aspect of healing. Those who come to understand it, experience it, and speak out of it declare a most unique message to the world: "I thank God for my suffering." Could anyone really say such a thing and mean it? The next chapter will explain why I think they can.

8

Revelation

*For this I bless You as the ruins fall: the pains You give me are
more precious than all other gains.*

— C.S. Lewis, *As the Ruins Fall*

In my deepest wound I saw Your glory – and it dazzled me.

— Augustine

Just beyond the thin walls of her hiding place, the young, smart, and terrified Immaculée Ilibagiza could hear the mob outside calling for her to come out and die. A hellish civil war that pitted the dominant Hutus against their Tutsi countrymen during the 1990s ravaged Rwanda, her once beautiful homeland. For Immaculée, the bloody genocide had come to this—a three-by-four foot bathroom space that hid her and seven other women from mobs on the prowl for Tutsi "cockroaches" to torment and kill.

Immaculée's improvised hiding place was in the home of a neighboring Hutu pastor. Hiding Tutsis in his house was extremely risky, but he hoped it would not be for long. Indeed, for eight people to endure a single day in such an impossibly small space would have tested anyone to the limits. "We were so exhausted, hungry, cramped and hot that our first day in the bathroom passed in a painful haze," Immaculée writes in her book, Left to Tell. "It was impossible to sleep—if I dozed off, I was immediately awoken by a leg cramp or someone's elbow knocking against my ribs."[1] How could they have guessed that circumstances would force them to endure these conditions for over three months?

When I first read Immaculée's descriptions of her ordeal, I was stunned by the magnitude of the challenges she endured while the world collapsed around her. But something else shines through her story. It is the way this unimaginable trial led her to experience the presence and power of God at a level far beyond anything she had ever known. Against all expectation the cramped bathroom that hid Immaculée from her would-be murderers turned out to be a portal of heaven.

But if heaven was close, hell was not far away. In addition to the relentless physical challenges, Immaculée also faced a growing spiritual battle with the hatred, fear and bitterness that threatened to take over her soul. A woman of deep faith, she instinctively knew that these things had the power to poison her the way they had her persecutors. She needed God to do the impossible within her own heart if she was to come through these trials whole.

Looking back, Immaculée describes her spiritual transformation while confined to her tiny bathroom hideaway: "I spent days with the word surrender, and I came to understand what it meant to surrender one's self to a Higher Power. I gave myself over completely to God. When I wasn't praying, I felt I was no longer living in His light, and the world of the bathroom was too bleak to endure."[2] In addition to her nearly ceaseless prayer life, she turned to the comfort, hope and guidance of the Bible—another gift from the Pastor who had been hiding her. Right away, she found this text from Psalm 92:

This I declare, that He alone is my refuge, my place of safety; He is my God and I am trusting Him. For He rescues you from every trap and protects you from the fatal plague. He will shield you with His wings! They will shelter you. His faithful promises are your armor. Now you don't need to be afraid of the dark anymore; nor fear the dangers of the day, nor dread the plagues of darkness, nor disasters in the morning.

"Though a thousand fall at my side, though ten thousand are dying around me, the evil will not touch me."[3]

With nowhere else to turn but God, Immaculée pressed deeper and deeper into into His presence. "I'd been praying continually for weeks, and my relationship with God was deeper than I ever imagined possible," she recalled. "That place was like a little slice of heaven, where my heart spoke to the Holy Spirit and the Holy Spirit spoke to my heart.

"I sat stone-still on that dirty floor for hours on end, contemplating the purity of His energy while the force of His love flowed through me like a sacred river. Sometimes I felt as though I were floating above my body, cradled in God's mighty palm, safe in His loving hand. In my mind, I heard myself speaking in exotic languages I'd never heard before—I instinctively knew that I was praising God's greatness and love."

After recounting these and other transcendent graces, Immaculée concluded:

> *Being in that bathroom had become a blessing for which I'd be forever thankful.* Even if my parents had perished in the bloodshed outside, I would never be an orphan. I'd been born again in the bathroom and was now the loving daughter of God, my Father. (*emphasis mine*)[4]

The first time I read her description of the bathroom as a blessing for which she would be "forever thankful," I was so taken aback that I dropped the book into my lap and let out an audible "Wow!" How, I wondered, could she say such a thing and really mean it?

Upon further reflection, it became clear to me that Immaculée was not praising the circumstances themselves, but the way God used them to catapult her more deeply into His presence. We see this critical distinction mirrored by the Apostle Paul in Romans 8. Nowhere in this passage does the apostle claim that all things are good (in and of themselves). Instead, he confidently asserts that "in all things God works for the good of those who love Him" (v. 8:8). In like manner, Immaculée was able to legitimately praise God for her ordeal because of how He worked through it. Her extreme need for God opened a door of revelation through which He stepped into her life. This is the heart of what I call "level five" healing.

The Greatest Healing

The fifth and final component of our healing model is the rarest and most remarkable. It is only available to people of faith—individuals who value the opportunity to know God above all else. This final dimension of healing is revelation.

People like Immaculée Ilibagiza, who walk in this dimension of healing, truly stand out. Of course, they speak with gratitude and joy about the repairs, recovery and redemption they have experienced. But they also value their defeats, weaknesses, limitations and needs. Why? Because every stop on the road to wholeness—from the highest mountain peaks to the deepest, darkest valleys—brought them face-to-face with the reality of God.

As opposed to shallow souls who flit from one spiritual fad to another searching for the next holy high, they are tethered to a more substantial faith. It is a faith informed not only by their spiritual peak experiences, but also by their pains, reversals, injustices and struggles. They have come to regard these things as teachers, friends and worthy companions for life's journey. Rather than overturning their faith, the trials and hardships they suffer tighten their grasp on grace.

The poet, Robert Brown Hamilton, captured this attitude in verse:

> I walked a mile with Pleasure
> She chatted all the way;
> But left me none the wiser
> For all she had to say.
>
> I walked a mile with Sorrow,
> And ne'er a word said she;
> But, oh! The things I learned from her,
> When sorrow walked with me.

Voices of faith through the ages testify to the rich treasures of God's presence to be found hidden beneath the rubble of life's most difficult experiences. One outstanding witness, the Apostle Paul, spoke openly of his delight: "In weaknesses (for the sake of Christ), in insults, in hardships, in persecutions, in difficulties. For when I am weak, then I am strong" (2 Corinthians 12:10). Ever since Paul first penned these words, voices of the faithful throughout the ages have picked up the refrain by adding their own "Amen".

But let's be realistic. I doubt many of us would willingly choose to endure intense trauma, hardships, injustices, sicknesses and the like, even if we suspect that doing so would bring spiritual benefits. Still, sometimes these things choose us. That's how life works when you're living in a sharp-edged world. There is, however, one choice we can make. It is whether we will allow our trials to make us bitter or better. That depends, at least in part, on how healed we want to be.

A Theology of Suffering

If you find it difficult to reconcile the presence of God with the reality of suffering, you're not alone. Great faith-filled minds have wrestled with such mysteries for centuries. It is often difficult, and sometimes just plain impossible, for us to make sense of suffering. What part does God play in the reality of the pain, injustice, illness, poverty, abuse, oppression and disease His beloved children experience in this life? Is He unsympathetic, lacking in power, enjoying some kind of cosmic tease? Inquiring minds want to know.

There are some who say God has nothing to do with suffering at all. We only have ourselves to blame. If we just had more faith or greater insight we would suffer far less. Others view suffering as punishment for our sins or misbehaviors. And of course there are those who consider an assignment of suffering as their "cross to bear" for His glory. While going through a particularly difficult time in her life, one friend of mine quipped: "The Lord must think that I can handle these trials, but I'm afraid He thinks way too highly of me!" Her comment reminded me of Tevye, the poor Jewish milkman from *A Fiddler on the Roof* who prayed in exasperation: "I know we are Your chosen people, but, once in a while, couldn't You choose somebody else?"

A hundred books on healing, faith and suffering could not resolve all these issues, much less the single volume now before you. However, in order the final level of healing to occur, two things need to be acknowledged:

1. Even the godliest people have been known to suffer.
2. In the midst of suffering, God is there.

The space between these two truths is occupied by the unique circumstances that make up each of our lives and, in this space, healing happens. Exactly how it happens is both a mystery and a marvel.

A Good Theology

A few years ago, I had the privilege of traveling through the beautiful country of New Zealand where I led healing ministry workshops at several Vineyard churches. Word of what I was doing reached a Christian radio station and they called me to arrange a live phone interview during one of their afternoon programs. It wasn't long before the interviewer posed the question: "If God still heals today as He did in Bible days, why isn't everyone healed?" It is a question that comes up often when the topic of divine healing is raised. As our conversation was broadcast across the nation, I decide to answer it as follows:

Part of the challenge of your question is that it is loaded. Some portions of the church are so focused on healing that they downplay suffering. Others focus so much on suffering that they dismiss healing. Everyone stakes out their own favorite territory around this question.

It would help us if we acknowledge that our theology of healing and suffering is shaped in part by our own expectations. Still, I believe it is impossible to have a good theology of healing if you don't have a good theology of suffering. In the same way, you can't have a good theology of suffering unless you have a good theology of healing. Each depends upon the other."

The five-dimensional model presented in this book helps in this regard since it is not an "all or nothing" approach to healing. This means we can acknowledge the healing we have already received while continuing to seek more. It also provides a way to acknowledge suffering and difficulty as part of the healing process instead of unrelated to it.

Maximum Healing

All healing is good healing no matter where we are in the process. There are choices we must make, however, about our willingness to cooperate with the healing work of the Holy Spirit. It is possible to limit healing to the relief of our symptoms (whatever they may be) and stop there. Or we can choose to continue the healing process, beyond the symptomatic level, into the deeper operations of God's grace. If we continue to say "yes" to God, the same grace that heals our symptoms will continue to draw us into a deeper knowledge of Him. In other words, we can take the healing and run, or we can approach our need for healing as an opportunity to better know our Healer. And this is the ultimate healing.

Notice how this worked in the biblical account of the 10 lepers healed by Jesus. In Luke we read:

As He was going into a village, ten men who had leprosy met Him. They stood at a distance and called out in a loud voice: "Jesus, Master, have pity on us!" When He saw them, He said: "Go, show yourselves to the priests." And, as they went, they were cleansed.

We might think that, given the incredible miracle these men experienced, all ten of them would return to Jesus afterwards. However, this was not the case:

One of them, when he saw he was healed, came back, praising God in a loud voice. He threw himself at Jesus' feet and thanked Him—and he was a Samaritan. Jesus asked: "Were there not ten cleansed? Where are the other nine? Was no one found to return and give praise to God except this foreigner?" Then He said to him: "Rise and go; your faith has made you well."

—Luke 17:12-19

Is there any doubt that the grateful Samaritan had a greater healing experience than the other nine men? While all received deliverance from their symptoms and were repaired in body, only he returned to reconnect with Jesus. But that's what grace does as we yield ourselves to it. It always draws us back to our Healer. By following grace into the presence of Jesus, the newly-healed man made the bond between them stronger. Now cleansed of his disease, he praised the Lord and thanked Him.

This man's actions remind us that we were born to know God, to experience Him and to love Him forever. It is in fulfilling this design that we are truly made whole. The leper had already been cleansed from his disease when Jesus told him to, "Rise and go; your faith has made you well." These words of blessing and affirmation were only spoken over the man who came back to Jesus after his cleansing. The other nine took their healing and moved on, missing out on the "more" they could have known. Let's not make that mistake.

I'm convinced that all our questions of healing and suffering will never be fully answered on this side of heaven. But that doesn't leave us with nothing. We may never know all the answers but we can know Him as the answer. We may never know all the "whys", but we can know Him as all-wise. We may never know His hidden purposes, but we can find His glory purposefully hidden in our deepest wounds, ready to shine forth and dazzle us. The Great Physician, it turns out, is also the Greatest Cure.

An Invitation

All other dimensions of healing are an invitation to this maximum healing that comes with a deeper knowledge of God (revelation). It's in the coming back to God, again and again, for all that He has for us that we experience wholeness. Remember the man Jesus healed by the Pool of Bethesda? Like the healed leper who reconnected with Jesus after his repair, this man also had an opportunity for a deeper encounter with the Lord. It happened at some point after he picked his mat up and walked away from the Pool of Bethesda as a new man.

Later, in the Temple court, Jesus approached the man again and made Himself known to him. Previously, the man could not say who it was who had made him whole by the Pool. But John reports that, after further interaction with Jesus, he "went away and told the Jews it was Jesus who had made him well" (John 5:15). What began as repair and restoration went on to become revelation.

Everything we receive from God provides an opportunity for us to develop a deeper relationship with Him. To know God is not only the maximum factor of healing, it is the maximum factor for life itself. "This is eternal life," Jesus prayed, "that they might know You, the only true God, and Jesus Christ, whom You have sent" (John 17:3). If our bodies worked better, our relationships were more solid, and our emotions were continuously stable and pleasant—and yet we did not get to know the Lord better—we would miss out on that which makes us truly whole.

Sadly, the evidence is that we too often behave like the nine missing lepers than the one who came back for more of Jesus. Dr. Karl Lehman, a psychiatrist with over 20 years experience, reports: "I have never had a person come to me with the request that I help them remove blockages so that they can have a closer relationship with Jesus." Recognizing this has inspired him to pray that those seeking his help will "pursue intimacy with Jesus as the primary purpose, and receive symptom relief as a pleasant side effect, instead of the other way around."[5] It seems to me that Dr. Lehman's approach is not only a more mature one, but more biblical as well.

How about You?

As you are reading this right now, you may have become aware that suffering has rocked your faith. You may have come to feel that, for some reason, healing is not for you. Your symptoms remain, your suffering continues and your struggles seem to be increasing. "Where is God?" you may ask. "Why won't He save me... rescue me... stop this pain... change my life?" On the surface, you may be doing your best to be strong and display faith, but inside you feel overlooked, disqualified and weak.

But what if healing was not an "all-or-nothing" proposition? What if God was at work through the very circumstances that try you most—those that call you to go deeper into His presence, to need Him more and to throw yourself into His fatherly arms with every last bit of your strength? What if that's where the healing was for you?

What if even death itself was just another opportunity to know Him better? If this was so, there would be nothing left to fear.

There are mysteries we must each explore and discover for ourselves. No two individuals have precisely the same story. "One-size-fits-all" is about socks, not life. Grace leads us each to God for salvation, through Christ, in ways that are never precisely the same. Each healing journey is driven by grace and is therefore unique. There are, however, three factors that can keep us pointed toward more.

9

Boldness

Whatever you can do, or dream you can, begin it. Boldness has genius, power and magic in it. Begin it now.

— Goethe

B oldness is powerful. By its very nature it is transformational, interruptive, challenging and catalytic. Indeed, a bold action or request can split a situation open like a watermelon, exposing a host of hidden possibilities.

Sometimes people fear approaching God with boldness. They are concerned that doing so will offend heaven's sensibilities. However, nothing in the New Testament tells us to hold back with God. On the contrary: robust and reverent boldness pleases God—He really likes it! (Hebrews 11:6) Indeed, we are urged to "approach the throne of grace with confidence, so that we may receive mercy and find grace to help us in our time of need" (Hebrews 4:16). A confident approach to the throne of grace finds its expression in a boldness of faith and an inward security that we will be received, not turned away. However, I admit that it takes practice to get bold faith right.

I'll never forget the time I boldly claimed healing for my dismal eyesight. It happened while I was still a teenager and a newly born again Christian. One day, while sweeping the driveway, my glasses accidentally fell off and shattered against the cement. In my spiritual immaturity, I took this as a sign that I should believe God for a healing of my poor vision. And why shouldn't I? The God I had come to know through Christ was powerful and compassionate. Furthermore,

I believed the Bible when it says that Jesus Christ, the great Healer, is "the same yesterday, and today and forever" (Hebrews 13:8). If these things were so, why couldn't I just claim my healing like I would a piece of luggage at the airport? Could there be a better time for a full-fledged healing than right after I ruined my glasses? I couldn't think of one.

There on the driveway, I composed a prayer of faith and thanksgiving in which I boldly accepted my healing in Jesus' name. Then, I opened my eyes and looked around. Nothing was different. My eyesight was just as bad as ever. Nevertheless, I refused to be discouraged. After all, I had heard somewhere that it was more important to maintain faith in God's promise to heal than to pay attention to what my "symptoms" were telling me. I determined to maintain my belief that I had been healed and carry on with my normal daily routine.

A couple of days later, while running an errand, I was waiting at a traffic light when a large Chrysler plowed into the back of my small imported car and pushed me out into the intersection. Thankfully there were no serious injuries, and before long a police officer arrived at the scene to make out an accident report. Checking my driver's license, he noticed that I was supposed to be wearing corrective lenses while driving. Naturally, he wanted to know what I was doing on the road without them. This, I thought to myself, was a perfect chance to boldly testify to my miraculous healing and bring glory to God. "I don't need to wear glasses, sir," I told him. "I've been healed."

Giving me one of those I'd-thought-I'd-heard-it-all looks, the officer pointed across the intersection at a license plate affixed to a parked car. "Read it," he said. I squinted. I strained. I silently prayed. Nothing. I could not make out a single letter or number. "Get some glasses," the officer said with a smirk as he handed me my driver's license and walked away. Suddenly, I felt foolish and ashamed at the poor way I had represented my faith and my Lord. My so-called healing was no great witness for Christ, that was for sure. In that moment, I began to understand that I still had a lot to learn about bold faith and how it really works.

Faith Versus Presumption

This experience was a major clue that there is a big difference between truly bold faith and my own presumption. I learned that I could not simply presume something upon God—even the powerful, merciful and generous God I had come to trust through Christ—and call it faith. Nor could I move God's hand by claiming a healing and then confessing it to be so. I have come to recognize that the only faith God honors is the faith He initiates. That's the way it worked in Bible days, and that's the way it works today. "I tell you the truth," Jesus said, "the Son can do nothing by himself; He can do only what he sees His Father doing, because whatever the Father does the Son also does" (John 5:19). If this was true for Jesus Christ, it is most certainly true for us.

Still, it would be a mistake to take a passive posture with God. The writer of Hebrews reminds us: "Without faith, it is impossible to please Him. For he that comes to God must believe that He exists, and that He rewards those who diligently seek Him" (Hebrews 11:6). And Jesus Himself counseled His disciples to "keep on asking and it will be given you; keep on seeking and you will find; keep on knocking [reverently] and [the door] will be opened to you; for everyone who keeps on asking receives; and he who keeps on seeking finds; and to him who keeps on knocking, [the door] will be opened" (Matthew 7:7-8, Amplified Bible).

What, then, are some of the things that distinguish authentic bold faith from foolish presumption? One of them has to do with origins. Presumption originates with me—my own efforts to "believe God." When compared to the gracious gift of faith that proceeds from God, my own self-generated attempts at showing faith are a real burden to sustain. Like a leaky balloon, my imitation faith must be continually "pumped up" with religious zeal and human effort or it will soon collapse.

By contrast, true faith is a gift from God—a gift of grace. Charles S. Price, a renowned healing evangelist from the 1940s, recognized this essential distinction when he wrote: "... I have beheld new beauties and glories of the Lord in the heart of that grace we call *faith*. I call it grace, because that is just what it is. In our blindness of heart and mind we have taken faith out of the realm of the spiritual and, without realizing just what we were doing, have put it in the realm of the metaphysical. An army of emotions and desires has driven Faith from the chambers of the heart into the cold and unfruitful corridors of the mind."[1]

Another thing that distinguishes faith from presumption is the ingredients that go into each of them. Presumption is two parts wishful thinking, two parts religious fervor and a dash or two of denial and manipulation. Faith, on the other hand, is 100% pure grace. Therefore, it has an energy all its own. It is undergirded by God's word, revealed by our fieriest trials, and it bears the pleasing and fruitful scent of heaven's aroma, rather than the rank odor of human effort.

We cannot manufacture this kind of bold faith. We cannot talk ourselves into it or otherwise conjure up the feelings that often go with it. As Price noted: "The thing above all else I want you to see is that you can not generate it; you can not work it up; you can not manufacture it. It is imparted and infused by God Himself. You cannot sit in your homes and struggle to have faith, and affirm that something is; nor can you turn your desire and hope into faith by your own power. The only place you can get it is from the Lord, for the Word clearly and distinctly states that faith is one of two things. It is either a gift of God, or it is a fruit of the Spirit."[2] Dr. Price's insights help us keep balance as we seek to be remain open to all God has for us without slipping into presumption.

Pushing Versus Walking

While ministering at a healing conference in England, I was approached by a woman who had been struggling to find the faith to overcome her agoraphobia—the so-called fear of public places. Those afflicted with this psychological, social impairment find it difficult to be out and about. If they do leave home, they are subject to the onset of uncontrollable panic attacks and other difficulties. It is a terrible way to have to live.

When she came to me for help, she told me that well-meaning Christian friends had been pressing her to believe the Lord for a breakthrough in her situation. If she would just believe and press through her fears she would certainly find release and deliverance once and for all. She tried to take their advice and push through by faith, but failed attempts to overcome her condition had only increased her sense of powerlessness and guilt.

I listened to her story and felt empathy for her long battle with the invisible enemy that had been holding her back for so long. Suddenly, in my mind's eye, I had a picture of Jesus standing by her front door in the entryway of her home (as I imagined it). He was waiting there for her to join Him for a walk.

"I believe the Lord is giving me a strategy to help you," I told her. "We're going to pray in just a moment but, before we do, I want you to promise me you'll try something when you go home. It's a whole different approach than what you've been trying.

"When you are at home, I want you to picture Jesus waiting in the entryway by your front door," I explained. "I want you to see Him standing there, ready to leave your home with you. Then, before you go out, I want you to ask Jesus to go with you as you leave. In fact, go on a little walk – just the two of you. Go only as far as you and Jesus decide to go. If it's only as far as the curb, that's fine. If it's around the block that's fine, too. Whatever you and Jesus decide together is how far you should go. Do you think you could try that?"

Her eyes lit up. "I believe I could," she replied. And, the next day, she did. In fact, she and Jesus went around her block together. She couldn't wait to get back to the meeting that night and tell me (another miracle, since the meeting was, obviously, a very public event). I rejoiced with her in her successful solo outing with Jesus and then I began to pray for her some more. After a few moments, I paused to ask her a question: "Can you recall when you first started feeling the fears that grew to become this agoraphobia in your life?"

She thought about it for a moment. "When I was a child, my parents would sometimes leave me in the care of my granny while they went out. In those days, we lived in a row house" (a tall, narrow structure with different living spaces on several different levels). "My room was up several flights of stairs and it was hard for my granny to go up and down them. So, when she would put me to bed at night, she would warn me that there were bogeymen and other horrible things that lived in the stairway at night and, should I get out of my bed or anything, they would get me." Suddenly, the root of her phobia became clear to us both.

It was time to ask Jesus to walk with her again—this time in to her past. In prayer, we asked the Lord to go with her back into the memories of her childhood home. We asked Him to show her how He was present with her in her bedroom and how caring and protective of her He was. We asked Him to go with her throughout the stair area of the home at night, side-by-side, and to cleanse her memories of the lies and horrors her granny had used to contain her in her room. We asked the light of God to fill that place through and through as she went through each room utilizing her sanctified imagination. Finally, we asked the Lord to give her the strength to forgive her granny for the sad, unwise and cruel method she chose for saving herself trouble with the stairs. As we concluded our prayer session, it was wonderful to sense the peace, grace and relief that had come to replace her anxious efforts to push herself through to freedom.

Boldness for Beginners

Many of us are not practitioners of boldness, especially boldness with God. I have heard preambles to prayers that go something like this: "Lord, you know that I haven't asked much of You lately, so if you could just …." or "God, if You're not too busy perhaps You could …" Our weak prayers and tentative approaches to God don't inspire us much to expect a strong answer. If we want to see what grace can really do, we have to pray differently. Confidently. Boldly. So how do we shift our prayer gears from *cautious* to *bold*?

Making It Practical

I recommend beginning by reacquainting yourself with biblical boldness. Below, I have listed some passages that underscore the way boldness with God is encouraged and rewarded according to the Bible. You may notice that I have already cited several verses of this kind in this chapter. I urge you to become well-acquainted with these and other biblical texts and even try praying through them using the language in the passage itself:

- Proverbs 28:1 – "The wicked flee when no one is pursuing, *but the righteous are bold as a lion*"
- Philippians 4:6 – "Do not be anxious about anything, but in everything, by prayer and petition, with thanksgiving, *present your requests to God.*"
- Matthew 7:11 – "If you, then, though you are evil, know how to give good gifts to your children, *how much more* will your Father in heaven give good gifts to those who ask Him?"
- Matthew 8:2,3 – "Lord, if You are willing, You can make me clean." Jesus reached out His hand and touched the man. "*I am willing*," He said, "Be clean!"
- Hebrews 4:16 – "*Approach the throne of grace with confidence*, so that we may receive mercy and find grace to help in our time of need.
- Hebrews 12:12,13 – "Therefore strengthen your feeble arms and weak knees. 'Make level paths for your feet' so that the lame may not be disabled, but rather healed."
- James 5:16 – "Therefore confess your sins to one another and pray for each other so that you may be healed. The prayer of a righteous man is powerful and effective."
- Jeremiah 17:14 – "*Heal me, O Lord, and I will be healed*; save me, and I will be saved, for You are the one I praise."

This list is not exhaustive. It is just a beginning. See what other verses you can find to add to it.

There is one bold prayer that has been prayed throughout the ages and throughout the church for hundreds of years. It is known simply as The Jesus Prayer. The Jesus Prayer is based on the text in Luke 18:10-14 (the story of the Publican and the Pharisee) and it goes like this:Lord Jesus Christ, Son of God, have mercy on me, a sinner. It is meant to be prayed repeatedly, over and over, as a way of centering one's heart on the mercy and grace of Jesus Christ. Some of the other texts I have highlighted could be prayed in a similar fashion.

Another way to appropriate more boldness in your approach to God is to read through the prayers the Apostle Paul prays for believers in Ephesians and Colossians. These are found in Ephesians 1:17–23, 3:16–21 and Colossians 1:10–14. Notice the confident nature of these prayers and how often and persistently Paul prays for them. They make an excellent guide to your own approach to bold prayer as you enter into the spirit of these prayerful passages.

How about You?

Are you hungry for more? Do you want more of God—more of His healing power, truth and light in your life? Are you sick of "barely enough" and ready to now "go bold?" Are you determined to pursue God boldly and steadily for what you need? Then what are you waiting for?

There is a holy boldness, a divinely-inspired desperation at the heart of the hungry. Notice how the Psalm-writer expresses it when he writes: "As the deer pants for streams of water, so my soul pants for You, O God. My soul thirsts for God, for the living God. When can I go and meet with God?" (Psalm 42:1-2). Perhaps these words could be your own. If so, you know you cannot live with the same-old-same-old. This means that you must be prepared to cast off religious self-effort and splashy displays of wannabe faith.

You have nothing to prove and no one you need to impress. The time has come to pay attention to the persistent tug of grace that is alive inside of you, calling you forward and leading you to Jesus and His mighty power. This is not about performing *for* God. This is about going *with God* into a future only He can make possible. It's about meeting Him at the door that leads to your tomorrows and stepping through it together, side-by-side as an act of absolute trust. But where will the Lord take you as you step forward? He will take you to where the healing happens. He will take you to a healing environment, the subject of our next chapter.

10

Environments

"Go," he told him, "wash in the Pool of Siloam" (this word means Sent). So the man went and washed, and came home seeing.

— John 9:7

Ricardo and I were friends for a couple of good reasons: he ran one of the best Mexican food restaurants in town and I love great Mexican food. Because my family and I ate there often, we enjoyed the kind of friendly relationship that sometimes develops between a restaurant owner and his "regulars." One particular evening, my family and I were savoring a typically delicious meal at Ricardo's place when he mentioned that one of his cooks, a young woman, had just burned her hand on the grill. "I'd like to pray for her," I quickly responded.

Given his religious tradition, I think Ricardo interpreted my statement to mean that I would offer up a prayer for her at church or perhaps during my own private devotions at home. I explained myself a little further: "What I mean is—if you're OK with this—I'd like you to take me back to the kitchen so I can pray for her healing." Clearly, this was new ground for Ricardo. Nevertheless, he invited me to follow him back into the kitchen work area.

A moment later we were standing near the hot grill with the young lady and one or two others from the cook staff. Acting as my interpreter, Ricardo introduced her to me in Spanish. He told her I was a friend and well-known customer who would like to pray for her injury. With Ricardo's help, I explained to her that I wanted to carefully place my hand on hers, in the area of the burn, and ask the Lord to heal it. After she nodded and held out her hand, I proceeded to pray for the burn area to be healed in Jesus' name. Specifically, I addressed the pain and swelling and asked God to quickly restore the affected area to normal. It only took a minute or two.

We finished praying and the young lady looked up at me with a smile. I wasn't sure whether or not her hand had improved after our brief time of prayer, but I was quite certain her heart had been touched. After thanking her for allowing me to pray for her, I left the kitchen and returned to my tacos. I doubt those seated nearby would have guessed that I had just come back from a back-room prayer meeting. Miraculously, however, God's love had temporarily transformed Ricardo's busy kitchen into holy ground. It was a good reminder of the way any place can be turned into a healing environment when the Holy Spirit is invited onto the scene.

Would you like to see more of God's healing power show up in the everyday places of your life? If so, there are two key concepts to grasp. First, recognize that all healing takes place within a healing environment. Second recognize that any place can become a healing environment. All it takes is a person of faith open to the possibilities that arise when the Spirit of God fills a particular place and time with His presence.

Creating a Healing Environment

Creating a healing environment can be as sophisticated as equipping a state-of-the-art medical facility with the latest hi-tech equipment or as simple as praying in the back room of a restaurant. That's because there are different kinds of healing environments for different kinds of needs. For example, each Thursday evening we open our church foyer to a local Alcoholics Anonymous group so they can use it for their weekly meeting. Within minutes, the leaders of this group build a healing environment out of some square footage, a coffee pot and some folding chairs. Then, after they have finished their meeting, the space goes back to being a plain old foyer again.

My church office is in a different part of the same building. When using this space as a private place to offer pastoral counseling or personal prayer it becomes another kind of healing environment. Down the hall is our church's main auditorium. While praying for the sick and ministering to the other expressed needs of our congregation during our Sunday worship services, it becomes yet another kind of healing environment. These various healing environments appear and disappear under the same roof each week, depending on the way our building gets used.

Of course, there are some healing environments that are special, dedicated spaces. The things that make them so are not always easily relocated to other environments. It would be prohibitive, for example, to strap a fully equipped operating room onto the back of a car and drive it over to the park to provide free surgeries for the homeless. On the other hand it is easy to turn a car, a park bench and a few square feet of grass into a healing environment with the help of some free groceries and an offer of prayer and care.

If we want to create healing environments for ourselves and others, we can begin by becoming aware of the transferable components that can turn any space into a healing place. Some of these transferable spiritual tools are obvious—faith, prayer, compassion, boldness, kindness, mercy and the presence and power of the Holy Spirit. Others, such as humility, truth, a sense of mission, worship, knowledge of God's word and a team of like-minded fellow healers can also radically reshape any environment into one that invites healing. If you sprinkle in a willingness to try something new, you'll find that opportunities for healing can pop up in the most unlikely places.

What about Gifting?

I didn't always see healing ministry like this. There was a time I assumed that God only heals when gifted people, functioning in a heightened religious environment, exercise their faith and spiritual expertise in a commanding way. This was the first model of healing ministry to which I was exposed as a teenager and new believer. Back then, I loved to hear the stories and read books that featured the spiritual adventures of my new healing heroes. Whenever I was able to watch a gifted healing evangelist in action (usually during a church service or dedicated healing meeting) I carefully took note of what they did so I could imitate them in my own small way. But these early experiences, while inspiring, also had a discouraging flip side. They reinforced my perception that I was not one of the mega-gifted.

Once I acknowledged this, I wasn't sure what to do. I really wanted the Lord to use me to bring healing to others. Furthermore, my study of the Bible convinced me that Jesus meant for His healing ministry to continue through His followers without interruption—even followers such as me. Still, I had no idea where to go or what to do in order to increase whatever healing gifts I might possess. It seemed that, when it came to healing and other gifts of the Spirit, either you had them or you didn't.

I was further perplexed by the vivid accounts of astounding personal visitations from God experienced by some high-profile healing personalities. It seemed that their unction to heal often came as a part of an extraordinary spiritual peak experience. All I knew was that God had never visited me in such dramatic ways and, even if He did, I would probably run for the hills rather than stick around to see what gifts He was passing out.

It's not that I doubted that at least some of these healing evangelists were for real. In fact, I still believe God chooses to release extraordinary gifts of faith through particular men and women for His glory according to His own plans and purposes. But I have noticed that our longstanding emphasis on giftedness has worked both *for* and *against* the spread of healing ministry among mainstream Christians. That is why I want to change our conversations about healing from ones that emphasize *healing gifts* to ones that emphasize *healing environments*.

By putting the focus on what we can do to create a particular healing environment, we put the spotlight where it belongs: on God, the Healer. Even people who feel less gifted than others can create healing environments into which they invite the power of the Holy Spirit to move. This is liberating to those who, like me, want God to use them in healing ways but may not feel supercharged with spectacular healing gifts. Remember: whether the setting is large-scale or intimate, temporary or permanent, medical, psychological, social or spiritual—all healing takes place in some kind of a healing environment.

If we concentrate on creating such environments, it releases us to look to God to do His part by filling these environments with all that He is. At that point, what actually happens to people, including ourselves, is up to Him.

One person who understands this better than just about anyone I know is my friend, Kathleen. As a dedicated Orange County sheriff's chaplain, Kathleen works alongside law enforcement officers and the coroner's office on the front lines of human need. Whenever she rolls on a call out, Kathleen knows she has to be prepared for the unknown. This has taught her to depend entirely upon God. "I know I can't do anything myself," she says. "I have to seek His presence wherever I might be."

The Ministry of Presence

As a chaplain, Kathleen understands she must provide what she calls *the ministry of presence*. This means, no matter what is going on around her; she must be present to people in need as a spiritual and practical asset. In order to effectively accomplish this, she knows she must first seek to tune in to the presence of God's Holy Spirit as she arrives on the scene. It is her awareness of His presence that gives her what she needs to fulfill her calling in a given situation.

There was the time, for example, when Kathleen was called out to the scene of a teen suicide in a highly affluent Southern California neighborhood. Working alongside the coroner, her attention was quickly drawn to the small crowd of terribly upset young people that had gathered there. Knowing they needed comfort and grace from above, Kathleen received the coroner's permission to ask them to join hands and unite with her in prayer. As she began to pray, she felt the presence of God increase. Before long, Kathleen became aware of specific things that God was giving her to speak out over several of the individuals in the circle. Later, a number of the young people shared with her how deeply they had been moved by this demonstration of God's mercy and love that showed up so richly on such a tragic scene.

On another occasion, Kathleen was called to the hospital bedside of a retired U.S. Marine Corps Major who was nearing death. Although he was normally a very private man, he trusted Kathleen and opened up to her during her visit. After being discharged to his home, he would sometimes page her and ask her to come by for a personal visit. During their talks together, they would review some of the remarkable life experiences that went with his military service and other things as well. Over time, their conversations also came to include the discussion of spiritual things. During one such discussion, this earthly warrior surrendered his heart to Jesus.

Soon afterward, Kathleen asked her dying friend if he had any regrets. "Just one," he responded. "I never took my family to church."

"All right," Kathleen replied. "Tomorrow is Sunday, so we'll just have church right here."

The next day, the Major's family arrived at his home dressed and ready for church. There was singing, readings from Scripture and a time of communion with bread and wine. Before dismissing everyone, Kathleen invited each of the Major's children to anoint their dying father with consecrated oil to give him their blessing. When it came time for his adult son to offer his dad a blessing, the young man broke out in sobs of repentance and openly asked for God to forgive and change him. This home-style church service was the first and last of its kind the Major and his family would share. By the middle of the following week the ailing soldier left this world to join his newfound Savior in glory to receive the ultimate healing—eternal life through Jesus Christ.

The Example of Jesus

No one could create powerful yet simple healing environments in everyday places as effectively as Jesus during the days of His earthly ministry. Two particular factors stand out when reading the gospel accounts of these events. One of them is *faith* and the other is *obedience*. On several notable occasions, Jesus commended people for their expressed faith in Him. In addition, He openly credited their faith as that which made them whole (Mark 5:34; Mark 10:52; Luke 17:19; Luke 18:42). By contrast, the widespread disbelief expressed by some of the people in Jesus' hometown was blamed for limiting His ability to do the miracles in that location during one of His visits.

(Matthew 13:58)

In addition to faith, the gospels also spotlight the way obedience to Jesus also brought a release of healing into the lives of certain individuals. One man was told by Jesus to wash out his blind eyes in a certain pool (The Pool of Siloam) as a part of his healing from blindness (John 9:7). There were times such as the one referenced in Matthew 9:6 when the Lord commanded someone who was paralyzed to, "Get up, take your mat and go home." When a company of 10 lepers approached Jesus to ask for healing from their disease, He responded by instructing them to go and present themselves to the Jewish priests. On their way to do so, their healing came (Luke 17:14). The man with the withered hand was instructed by Jesus to first stretch it out. As he did so, it was made as whole and functional as his other hand (Mark 3:5). Simple acts of faith. Simple acts of obedience. Mighty works of power.

Whether it involved clearing out noisy mourners so He could quietly bring Jarius' daughter back to life (Luke 8:49-56), or healing a blind man along the roadside (Mark 10:46-52), Jesus brought healing to the places people lived their real lives. With Jesus on the scene, Simon Peter's home (Luke 4:38-39), a Pharisee's home (Luke 14:1-4), Zacchaeus' house (Luke 19:2-8), and a synagogue (Mark 3:1-4) all became sites of healing grace during those days. Is there any reason, then, why a business office, a church service, a gas station or a neighbor's back yard couldn't be places where healing happens today?

Creating a Healing Environment for Yourself and Others

Faith and obedience continue to be the keys to creating healing environments in our time, just like they were for Jesus and His disciples. Faith focuses us toward God and what only He can make possible. Obedience is the "me" part. If we wish to help others or ourselves into a deeper encounter with the Lord, our goal should be to increase the God-ward flow of faith along with our own willingness to do whatever He asks of us. An environment, no matter how mundane, that is filled with faith and obedience is an environment rich with divine possibilities.

The kind of healing faith we see on display in the New Testament is often raw, emotive and even primal in its expression. It is "gut faith" more than "head faith". That isn't to say it has no intellectual component. Rather, it is to point out that healing faith is not a matter of intellectual assent alone, but of deep-seated hope placed in God.

In the healing environments I have been in (both private and corporate), this kind of faith shows up in a mental, spiritual and even physical posture of invitation, welcoming and openness to the felt presence and power of God. Such faith moves me to surrender my need to control outcomes. I yield to God and place myself in His Bigger Hands as if I was going to receive a gift rather than earn a reward. Outwardly, it might be expressed in kneeling, lying face down, lifting my hands in surrender or opening them as if I was going to be given something. The upward flow of faith quiets my mind and dials down my anxious concerns. I breathe slower. My head lifts. I let out a sigh. I am His and His alone.

Worshipful music and singing, whether live or recorded, elevates my sense of adoration, surrender and expectancy. The reading or teaching of God's word inspires me to hope in Him and to believe Him for all that I need. My attitude moves to one of "anything can happen, anything is possible with God." This springs me free from my default mode of limited expectations and mini-possibilities. Consequently, I move toward God—seeking Him and whatever He has for me in that moment with gratitude and receptivity.

How about You?

Have you also questioned the level of your spiritual giftedness? Has doing so led you to disqualify yourself as a practitioner or receiver of healing prayer ministry? Have you dismissed the possibility of God doing remarkable things in everyday settings either in yourself or others? Have you criticized yourself as being of "little faith" because you have found it hard to believe that God will completely make you whole all at once? If so, I urge you to take a new approach to your healing and wholeness. Rather than focusing on giftedness or a single healing event, try creating a variety of healing environments where you can and put yourself into them. You may also receive great benefits by visiting dedicated healing environments created by other believers such as healing prayer services, small group prayer meetings, deeply inspirational worship environments and the like.

Begin in your home, your car, your office lunch hour or while the kids are swinging on the swings at the playground. Stop. Pause. Quietly sing a hymn or song of love and praise to the Lord—even if no one else on earth hears it besides you and Him. Invite the Holy Spirit to come to wherever you may be. Welcome Him to rest upon you, fill you, and permeate your deepest being—the way sweet rain soaks into sun-parched soil. Read or recite the promises of God you find in the Bible. Meditate upon them. Open yourself to the truth you find in the timeless, living words of Scripture.

If you are able to gather with a few others, try building this kind of environment together. It doesn't need to be "professional" or highly-structured. Simple is good. In this setting, spend some time singing worship songs and reading scripture passages out loud. Begin with adoration, shedding your daily distractions. Make room for the Spirit-inspired confession of sinful attitudes or actions and the prayers of repentance and forgiveness that follow. Having emptied yourself of your usual anxieties, frustrations, agendas and busyness in these ways, you will be more open to God's voice, His inspirations, His healing touch and His motivating grace.

Focus on what Jesus has already done for you—on what His life, death, resurrection and kingly authority make possible. Meditate, for example, on the meaning of this passage from the book of Hebrews:

Therefore, brothers, since we have confidence to enter the Most Holy Place by the blood of Jesus, by a new and living way opened for us through the curtain, that is, His body, and since we have a great high priest over the house of God, let us draw near to God with a sincere heart in full assurance of faith, having our hearts sprinkled to cleanse us from a guilty conscience and having our bodies washed with pure water.

Let us hold unswervingly to the hope we profess, for He who promised is faithful. And let us consider how we may spur one another on toward love and good deeds.

— Hebrews 10:19-24

Utilizing the laying on of hands, pray for one another for healing, restoration, redemption, repair, removal of that which causes injury and a greater revelation of God in each of your lives. Be specific. Be gentle. Be considerate. Be bold. Pause again. Listen to God and to one another. Take time. Bless what you see already taking place and continue until you sense God is directing you to stop for now. Some refer to this kind of experience as "soaking prayer". Those words aptly describe what takes place in a session like this—soaking in the Lord, in His word, in His worship and in the healing prayer and love of His people. Do it regularly, repeatedly and as much as is reasonably possible.

Finally, I urge you to take whatever faith, obedience and love that you find within you and use these things to build healing environments in everyday places for others. One friend of mine tells me his secret: "I ask people how they are doing and then I listen to their response *as if it really mattered to me*." This, he tells me, has opened up many opportunities for personal ministry along life's highways and byways.

In order to boldly press forward in faith and obedience, you will need the help and encouragement of others. In the next chapter, I will help you rediscover the greatest healing environment on earth. It is the living community of God's people: the Church.

11

Community

A central task of community is to create a place that is safe enough for the walls to be torn down, safe enough for each of us to own and reveal our brokenness. Only then can the power of connecting do its job. Only then can community be used of God to restore our souls.
— Larry Crabb, *The Safest Place on Earth*

Dear Church,

I am writing this to let you know that I have thought a lot about breaking up with you recently. You've probably felt me running hot and cold and wondered what was up. I apologize for not being more open with you sooner. Frankly, I find it hard to be honest about my ambivalence towards you because I owe you a lot. You taught me where I came from as a believer and where I'm going. You taught me to take risks with my spiritual gifts. You gave me an environment that allowed me to explore everything from worshipping God to raising children. I can't thank you enough. Still, there are some things I need to say if we are to go on.

See, I'm torn because the best people I have ever known—the people who I most want to be like and have most inspired me—are in my life because of you. That's undeniably true. But it's also true that you have also introduced me to the people who have brought me the most disappointment, the most heartache and the most embarrassment. I'm just not sure what to make of that. You have wounded me, but you have also healed me. Clearly, Church, you are capable of both.

That's why some things have got to change between us. I know that I can't be whole without you. I can't heal in isolation. I can't see clearly without the eyes you give me. I can't experience the give and take of God's kingdom without being up-close-and-personal with you. I need you and you need me. I get that. But we've got to stop pretending that we are close when we're not.

For example, I can't stand the way you tell me that I need to be intimate and honest with you and then punish me for doing so. If you really want me to go there, you have to model that for me—act like it really matters. You tell me how important it is to confess my sins in order to be healed. Fine. But how am I supposed to do that in a class, a program or a crowd? Even my "small group" is just another place where this *almost* happens, but not really. In other words, I need you to stop teasing me about all this "community" you keep talking about and show me what sacrifices you're willing to make for it to really happen.

And here's another thing: how can I drop my guard, come clean and invite others to do the same when you constantly promote "having it all together through Jesus" as normal? Sure, some of these stories inspire me, but so often you make it sound like it all just happens by magic. Doesn't transformation require life-on-life relationships between sincere believers? Why can't you just say so? Don't tell me I have to leave you in order to find the *real* you I've always wanted. That would be just too sad.

Look, I'm willing to give it another try. There's still no one else like you. You have been endowed with the Word and the Spirit. You still tell God's saving story. And when you get it right, you *really* get it right. But I'm asking you to make some big changes and to make them as quickly as possible. I need to do more than "go on a date" with you once or twice a week. I need us to really hang out together. Let's not just "do lunch", let's "do life." Are you up for this? I certainly hope so. If not, I can't imagine where I'm going to find what only you and I can share.

So, think it over—but not for too long. The clock is ticking and I'm not getting any younger—and, by the way, neither are you.

Yours Truly,
Bill

* * *

Healing Happens in Community

Have you ever wanted to write a letter to the Church? Not necessarily a particular church, but the Church as a whole. If so, what would you ask for in your relationship with her? Slicker programs? More impressive buildings? A greater number of classes, Bible studies and sermons? Or is there something inside of us that cries out for *community*—common ground—connections that invite reality? I suspect that many who want greater healing and wholeness desire church relationships of that kind. That's because we've probably figured out by now that healing doesn't only happen in our solo walk with the Lord. It also takes place through the give-and-take of our relationships with others in the kingdom of God.

Becoming as "healed as can be" requires life-on-life relationships with those whom God gives us to be in relationship with. We need them and they need us. Without each other, we are like surgeons trying to operate on ourselves. By contrast, when we really stand together and fight for each other, we are *powerful*. In fact, I'm continually surprised by the way God uses us to heal each other—even when we don't know it!

A Hidden Healing

A particularly unforgettable experience of what might be called a "hidden healing" took place during a conference for Christian singles I was in charge of. It was the first morning of this three-day event and things were off to a great start. As we gathered for that morning's opening worship time, I found myself deeply inspired by the atmosphere of music, celebration and devotion swirling around me. Everyone from the musicians on the platform to those of us in our seats seemed to relish the liberty and joy we were feeling in our hearts that day.

Before long, I became aware that the line between "musicians" and "audience" had become blurred by the presence of God in that place. It was clear that all of us had somehow become "the worship team". While the musicians skillfully played their instruments at the front of the room, the rest of us joined in with voices and upraised hands giving glory and love to the Lord. It was in that moment that I suddenly got the inspiration to try something I had never tried before. Between songs, I got everyone's attention and began to quickly reorganize the entire room.

While the musicians waited, all 100 people moved to the front of the stage area and joined them. Taking our places on the long steps in front of the band, we were an ad hoc choir. This new room arrangement reinforced the timeless truth that while the church is at worship God alone is the only "audience" that really matters. Having become settled in our new configuration, we faced the now empty seats and joined the musicians as we continued the morning's praise and worship together.

As the music swelled, my ears caught the sound of an exceptionally beautiful female voice coming from somewhere nearby. After listening more closely, I determined that it belonged to a young woman who was standing on the step just below me and to my left. "Wow", I thought, "I've got to get her to a microphone."

While the music continued, I got the attention of the lead musician. We quickly worked out a way for a microphone to be made available to the newly-discovered singer and I returned to my spot on the steps. Leaning forward, I tapped the young lady on the shoulder so I could invite her to join the band. She appeared a bit startled when she turned and saw that it was me who wanted to speak with her. "Your voice is beautiful," I told her, and then I then urged her to go up and sing into the open mike.

"You want me to sing?" she asked. "Up there?

"Yes, I arranged for you to join them."

Convinced at last that she had heard me correctly, she moved up by the musicians and sang into the microphone for the remainder of the morning's worship.

Later, as the session came to a close and people were milling about, I noticed this same young woman walking toward me. She introduced herself and asked if we could speak more privately. After stepping a few feet from the crowd, she began to tell me her story.

"You'll never know what this morning meant to me."

"Great," I said in my best pastoral tone. "I'm glad to hear it".

"No, you don't understand," she said as her eyes welled up with tears. "A few years ago, I was a worship leader back in my home church. At the time I was married and had a family. But I made a huge mistake. I had an affair with a married man who led worship at another church." She paused to regain her composure.

"Once everything came to light, it broke up both our families. Of course, we were each asked to step down from our roles by the leaders of our churches. From there things just got worse." She paused again, and then continued. "I felt like my whole world was falling apart," she told me. "We soon broke off our relationship for good, and I tried to go back and make things right with God and with the people I had hurt. But it's been really hard. I haven't been able to forgive myself for what I did with all the blessings and gifts God has given me. I have pretty much hated myself ever since."

As I listened, my heart went out to her. I wanted to respond, to help her unload her burden of guilt and self-loathing. But before I could respond, she said something I will never forget.

"When you tapped me on the shoulder this morning, my first thought was that someone had told you about me and that you were going to ask me to sit down."

I couldn't believe what I was hearing. *Is that who she thought I was? Is that who she thought she was—a candidate for public shaming?*

"Before today, I had concluded that God never wanted to hear my voice in church again," she sobbed. "But, when you got my attention this morning, you didn't ask me to sit down. You told me my voice was beautiful and that I should go up and sing with the band *into the microphone.* You'll never know what you did for me today. God used you to let me know I am truly forgiven. Now I know I can be restored. I will never be able to thank you enough."

Nothing she could have told me would have surprised me more.

Reflecting on my experience with her later, two things stood out to me. One was how amazing it was that God would use me to deliver a message of mercy and restoration to someone without my even knowing it. The other was how stubborn the guilt and shame she had been laboring under had become until her moment of freedom arrived. While I was certain that I would not have asked her to sit down had I known about her past, I had to admit I wasn't entirely sure I would have invited her to step up to the mike. That's because *my* mercy is limited. But His mercy is immeasurable. Without our realizing it, His Spirit had set up a scenario in which she could receive a hidden healing neither of us would ever forget. God designed His people to be a worshiping and serving community of healing grace. This is the church at its best.

A Healing Community

Although the church is meant to be an environment in which people can find wholeness of body, soul and relationship through God's mercy, grace and truth, it is not perfect. Even the New Testament portrays the church of the First Century as anything but problem-free. Nevertheless, the Bible writers celebrate the church as the called-out community of God on earth. It was not established on trends, fashions, self-help, or the shifting sands of popular opinion but on the foundation of Jesus Christ and His apostles and prophets (Ephesians 2: 20). Note the high view of the church expressed in the following passage from the book of Hebrews: "You have come to Mount Zion, to the heavenly Jerusalem, the city of the living God. You have come to thousands upon thousands of angels in joyful assembly, to the church of the firstborn, whose names are written in heaven" (Hebrews 12:22-23a).

The Bible asserts that God has invested the church with His Holy Spirit—the true source of healing grace and power. It is founded upon the perfect life, death and resurrection of His Son, Jesus. He alone is the God-sent Savior and Healer of the human condition who "... went about doing good and healing all who were under the power of the devil, because God was with Him" (Acts 10:38). No other institution on earth has been thus endowed.

I'll admit there are times I feel ashamed of the church. Yet in my heart I know God is not ashamed of her. He is, in fact, her Champion. This is vividly described in the opening chapters of the book of Revelation wherein John sees a vision of Jesus walking in the midst of the churches. The Lord makes it clear that He is intimately aware of their secrets and shortcomings as well as their triumphs and strengths. Yet, even as He brings strong words of correction, He ceaselessly urges her to reach for her highest and greatest potential. Without a doubt, He is with her in her trials and strongly believes in her ultimate overcoming power.

Even the Apostle Paul, who knew better than most how frustrating church leadership could be, asserts that God has put the church on display as a living trophy of His wise workmanship. "Through the church," Paul writes, "the complicated, many-sided wisdom of God in all its infinite variety and innumerable aspects might now be made known to the angelic rulers and authorities (principalities and powers) in the heavenly sphere" (Ephesians 3:10, Amplified Bible). If God can afford to brag to the cosmos about the church, we might try a little harder to be affirming of her as well.

Where's the Healing

The scriptures make it clear that God has raised up the church to bring glory to Him, life to its members and a lasting witness to the world. So how did the church lose its identity as a place of exceptional healing grace? In his book, *The Nearly Perfect Crime*, author Francis MacNutt blames this phenomenon on a long-term conspiracy hatched in hell:

> "The Church's original healing ministry was so strong and vital, so clearly a part of the Gospel, that the crime (robbing the church of its healing ministry) could not take place all at once. It took time – nearly two thousand years."[1]

The good news is that the execution Francis MacNutt refers to as "the nearly perfect crime" was cut short thanks to the revival of Christian healing ministry over the past several generations. He points out that much of this renewal of interest in healing has taken place among ordinary people, apart from the influence of theological experts or church authorities. The result is a ground-up renovation of the church's purpose and identity for our times.

Since healing grace requires an environment of faith, honesty and mercy; dead traditionalism and stifling church professionalism must run their course before the flame of healing will fully reignite. Nevertheless, the more recent rediscovery of the church's call to authentic community has added even more fuel to the fire of healing renewal. As a result, there is a new vitality in the church that is finding expression through acts of healing, transformation, belonging, compassion and restoration. Remarkably, this fresh wind of the Spirit has largely circumvented longstanding controversies of high church versus low-church, Catholic versus Protestant, or "old-school" versus "cutting edge" church forms. Instead, issues of healing in the church center more on whether a rising appetite for God, deepening hunger for wholeness and increasing confidence in the Bible will be nourished within a given faith community.

Turning Chairs

If we wish to see the level of healing rise in our various church environments, then the biblical admonition from the Apostle James to "confess your sins to one another and pray for each other so that you may be healed ..." must be taken seriously. Author Larry Crabb believes this cannot happen if our idea of church life is to sit behind one another in tidy rows, isolated and uninvolved, Sunday after Sunday. We must, he insists, turn our chairs around and face one another if the church is ever to ever truly be the church. This, he hastens to remind us, is not without its challenges:

"When we move beyond simply wanting people to show up for church, to support the budget, and to do nothing publicly immoral or disruptive, when we enter people's lives and see what the inside struggles are, we feel confused. And often disappointed."[2]

Nevertheless, he insists we must press through the inevitable discomforts of living truthfully before each other if we want the real thing:

"I am radically pro community. I believe that under the terms of God's new covenant with humankind, the Holy Spirit has graciously placed resources in every Christian that, when released from one person and received into another, can promote substantial healing and change. A connecting community, where each member is joined together in dynamic spiritual union, is a healing community."[3]

Some of us have moved our chairs away from the church in an attempt to avoid its faults and treacheries. Sitting alone as a "church of one" may solve some short term problems, but it is a long-term recipe for spiritual dryness and ineffectiveness. We're kidding ourselves if we think we don't need one another in order to experience wholeness and finish well.

Others of us prefer our church chairs to be firmly set into tidy, impersonal rows. This provides the illusion of "belonging" to one another even as we remain fundamentally unknown and unknowing. Many church-goers think this is sufficient. For those who want to be as healed as can be, however, it will never do. We are the ones who, while trembling, have taken the risk of turning our chairs to face each other for real. Refusing to trivialize the biblical terms *brother* and *sister*, we have allowed our fellow believers to become a significant part of our lives and they have asked the same of us. Is this risky? Without a doubt. Is it the path to deeper healing? Without question.

There is more than one way to create more intimate Christ-centered relationships but one of the ways I have "turned my chair" towards my Christian brothers has been to participate in a so-called Power of Four group. Along with three other men from my church, I have chosen to share my ups and downs, my counsel and my confusion, my prayers and my panic while also allowing the other guys to share their lives with me. Some fellow pastors have told me I'm crazy for taking such risks with members of my flock, but I emphatically insist it is those who lack a circle of intimate Christian relationship that are most at risk. I have come to echo the words of one of the men in my group who asserts: "I could not be the man I am today but for the men God has put in my life."

Whether it is by tapping into the Power of Four or by some other mode of intimate Christ-centered relationships, our further healing will depend on connecting with trusted fellow believers for real.

12

Roadmap

I'll march this road, I'll climb this hill
down on my knees if I have to
I'll take my place upon this stage
I'll wait 'till the end of time for You
like everybody else

— The Call, "I Still Believe"

While traveling through England, I met a man with an unusual hobby. He told me he liked to drive his small car off the main highway deep into the English countryside. Then, after going as far into the backcountry as possible, he would try to find his way back to the highway without using a map. This might be a fun way for some people to spend a weekend, but it would never do as a technique for running an ambulance service. It's interesting, then, to note how often the road to wholeness feels more like a meandering trip down a backcountry road than it does a blast down the highway in the back of a speeding ambulance. But is it really as random as all that? I think not.

While I know of no one-size-fits-all template for the way God works in each of our lives, there are features of the healing process we can all become familiar with and make use of as we go forward. These are the starting places, landmarks and mile markers that can help us find our way. By taking note of them, we can better understand where we have come from, where we are now and what lies ahead. Our goal, then, will be to see if we can put together a roadmap of our own.

Start Here

Of course, I am assuming that you have answered "yes" to the question, "Do you want to be healed?" I'm also assuming the question, "How healed do you want to be?", has inspired you to pursue more of the wholeness God has for you. But if you have not yet resolved these two key questions, I urge you to go no further until you do. If, however, you have dealt with them decisively, the next thing is to tell someone about it. Ideally, the person you inform is someone important to you—someone who can pray for you, support you, encourage you and perhaps even prod you forward when you get stuck. Who do you know like this? A priest, pastor or small group leader? A friend or a spouse? A counselor, advisor or spiritual director? Whoever it is, your message should be something like this:

> I am committing to change. I want to be whole and I'm reaching for it with everything I've got. I have no intention of stopping at the surface level. I'm going for all the deep healing God has for me. I do not ever intend to quit.

Something powerful happens when we tell others what we are committed to. Our words define and redefine us as we go through life. This is plain to see as we witness wedding vows, say the pledge of allegiance or answer questions in a courtroom. Even our spiritual commitments are empowered when we go "on the record." The Apostle Paul, for example, says that if you "confess with your mouth, 'Jesus is Lord', and believe in your heart that God raised Him from the dead, you shall be saved" (Romans 10:9). Of course in all of these matters, we must mean what we say. Empty words are weak. But words spoken aloud with conviction and filled with meaning have the power to launch us into a new orbit. Who is first on your list to tell?

Point of Reference

By telling someone about our commitment to be healed, we automatically identify a starting point from which we can then measure our progress. Every trip has a beginning, including the one that will take you to the future God has in store. You may be making an entirely new start. You may be starting over. Or you may be starting a new phase of a journey already begun. In any case, it is vital that you take some time to clearly identify square one.

Recovery programs such as Alcoholics Anonymous (AA) understand the importance of identifying a starting point and marking progress from there. In AA, a small medallion or "chip" is used to celebrate various periods of successful sobriety. The chips are presented after 30 days, 90 days, six months, one year, and so on. These chips are small objects with a big purpose—they are mile-markers on the road to new life. Other physical objects can serve a similar purpose. For example, take the way the people of Israel utilized a pile of stones to mark their miraculous new beginning as a nation in the Promised Land.

The Old Testament book of Joshua describes how the people of Israel arrived at the banks of the Jordan River following decades of wilderness wanderings. To cross fully into the Promised Land, they needed only to get safely to the other shore. Miraculously, God opened a dry passage through the Jordan for His people to cross through. As they did, their leader Joshua instructed them to collect 12 rocks from the dry riverbed to be stacked as a memorial when they reached the other side. This monument was meant to serve as a perpetual reminder of God's faithfulness to bring His people all the way to their destination (Joshua 4:6-22). What a remarkable example for us to learn from as we seek to cross over into a new life in Christ!

There is, in fact, no limit to the creative ways you may choose to mark your new beginnings and subsequent progress. It can be done with something as small and simple as an AA chip or as elaborate as a new house, new job or new city. If you enjoy writing, you may prefer to keep a running journal, diary or blog. I have also known people to memorialize their new start with a tasteful tattoo! The possibilities are endless.

Some time ago, I helped a young woman create a ceremony to mark a new beginning in her life. It was designed to help her move forward after an important relationship came to a painful end. The date of the ceremony, July 27, was designed to coincide with the date her relationship ended a few years before. Ever since then, she had been consumed by that anniversary to the point of obsession. Even the numbers 7-2-7 on the face of a digital clock could trigger the memory of her loss.

The ceremony we designed to be simple enough for her to share with a few friends, but effective enough to unhook her obsession with lost love. Once the day arrived, she and her friends met at a pre-selected outdoor site. As they gathered around her, she told them the story of her relationship and the painful way it ended. She also explained that she was determined to reclaim that date, July 27, from its association with sorrow and loss in order to recast it as a day of victory and new life. Following this, she dug a hole in the ground and placed some papers and letters into it—remembrances of things past that had, by this time, become a burden to her—and lit them on fire.

As the flames consumed these mementos, she and her friends joined hands to pray for God's healing, mercy and forgiving power. Afterward, she read some scripture passages aloud and then finished the ceremony by placing a few other small non-combustible items in the hole before filling it with dirt again. A closing time of prayer and worship followed. Then, arm-in-arm, she and her friends turned and left. She later reported that, from that day forward, the ceremony had successfully changed the way she thought about July 27 for good. It had shifted from being a reminder of unresolved hurt to a celebration of healing, friendship, God's faithfulness and more. It was the starting point of a new beginning.

The Journey Continues

Once you have designated your starting point and begun to move forward, it is important to become aware of your surroundings just as if you were using a map to guide you through an unfamiliar city. That's why we will now take some time to briefly revisit the five aspects of healing outlined at some length in the middle portion of this book. As you review their various features you can better identify where you are on the map as you press forward in your commitment toward greater wholeness.

Before looking at them more closely, remember that each one should not be treated as if they were isolated rungs on a ladder.

Instead, think of them as zones of experience with "soft" borders. At any particular time, we are likely to be dealing with issues related to more than one of them. Still, in a general sense, one does lead to another over time. The following questions are designed to help you assess which zone you are most involved with at present and where your future healing lies:

Removal

• Am I still living out of my pain, injury, disability or disease as one of the "walking wounded"? To what extent has that which has caused me injury been addressed and removed?

• What evidence can I point to that demonstrates the removal of the source of my injury? Can others see a change in me? Do I feel unburdened, resolved or free of issues or conditions that had been draining or impairing me?

Repair

• What evidences of repair do I see in my life or my situation? What now "works" that didn't used to?

• In what ways am I less vulnerable to being re-injured? What new boundaries have I established? What treatments have I successfully undergone?

• How am I eating, sleeping, relating and functioning in ways that are no longer defined by brokenness? What new habits, people, routines and reports give evidence to the repair or repairs I have undergone?

Restoration

• What have I reclaimed or found that I feared had been lost for good?

• Where do I stand with the "big questions" of my life—the "whys and wherefores" of my situation? How aware am I of the presence of God?

• What am I celebrating these days? What do I have left to mourn? Has the level of heartfelt gratitude and praise risen in my life? In what concrete ways am I expressing this?

Redemption

• Can I identify specific ways God is transforming my reversals into something that could actually bring about good?

• Has my focus shifted towards the needs of others? What needs and challenges faced by others am I now more aware of than I used to be? What are some ways I have thought of helping?

Revelation

• Have I come to the place where I can sincerely say aloud: "I thank God I had to go through my situation or condition because of the way it brought me to a deeper knowledge of Him?"

• Have I been able to return to an unpleasant or devastating time, place, memory or experience in my life and convert it into a point of worship?

The Vanguard

Answering some of these questions will require little effort while others will demand that you struggle. The ones that stretch you reveal where the cutting edge, or vanguard, of your faith is. In military terms, a vanguard is the part of the army that leads the rest of the troops into battle. The vanguard is the first to contact the enemy, meet the obstacles and find the opportunities. Therefore, the vanguard plays a vital role in the ultimate outcome of the fight.

For the entire army to function as a vanguard would be impractical and possibly destructive. In addition to a cutting edge, a well-organized army also has a main body ready to come up from behind and move the battle forward. In the same way, the faith that leads you into a healing experience has both a leading edge and a main body. It is important to know one from the other if you wish to stay present to all the healing possible. So, how do you distinguish between them?

It's not difficult, really. The vanguard of your healing is the point at which your faith is most stretched, your challenges are greatest and your hopes for the future are most poignantly felt. It is your high risk, high reward zone. When Jesus commanded the man by the Pool of Bethesda to get up and walk, He was calling forth the vanguard or leading edge of the crippled man's hopes, faith and expectations.

Although the man had no natural reason to try and push on his lifeless legs, he did so anyway. What followed behind this vanguard of obedient response to Jesus was the main body of the man's miraculous healing. That's life on the edge.

We cannot live "on the edge" of our faith all the time. However, there is a part of our faith that is always being challenged to press into the possibilities and confront the obstacles that keep us from wholeness. Where does that leading edge lie for you right now? It is not your comfort zone—the place where you are able to call the shots. It's just beyond that, where it would take a miracle for things to be different in your life. It is the tip of the arrow that is flying into your future, not the arrow itself. To be in touch with the vanguard of your faith is to be in the place where visions, possibilities, dreams, hopes and alternatives are nurtured in a sacred space—one that lies between the presence of God and your mind, body and soul. If there is no cutting edge, no place of high risk and high reward, then your faith life will feel lifeless, flat and blunt.

It's hard on the edge. To go there is to push on the possible and insist that it give way. I have a hundred vivid memories of Robin in that place as she has pressed into her post-crash future. There have been days upon days of physical therapy where even the simplest task required her to tolerate excruciating levels of pain. There were the occasions of her first solo shower, her first time back up the stairs of our house, her first time behind the wheel of a car again, her re-enrollment in school to finish her degree and her return to work at a hospital.

Without an edge, there's no place where a different future can find formation. Where is your vanguard? What is it that you are courageously taking on, boldly attempting and prayerfully pushing into? If you don't have one, it's time to find one. If you have lost one, it's time to get it back again. If you have one, keep it sharp. This is where the action is!

How about You?

Now it's time to put the pieces together. You've made the decision to go for deeper healing and shared this decision with someone important to you. You've identified your starting point so that your progress can be measured. You have revisited the five aspects of healing so that you have a clearer sense of which zone you are working in most. And, you have given definition to your personal high risk/high reward zone—the cutting edge of your faith and the gateway to your preferred future. You have begun to draw your roadmap. As you continue toward wholeness, you will need to refine and redraw your personal map as new insights, understanding, progress, challenges and reversals arise.

Each healing journey is different, each one unique. For some it involves recovery from an accident, a battle with cancer or other disease, or a debilitating addiction. For others, it is about coming back to life after the stunning loss of a loved one or envisioning a new life after a divorce or separation. No two stories are quite the same.

I have shared our story and the stories of others to give you inspiration, information and preparation for the journey that lies before you. Now you must decide whether or not you will move forward into the future with faith or fear. There is no guarantee of earthly success. Even those bodies Jesus healed and raised from the dead eventually returned once again to the dust from which they came. That's why I'm glad that Jesus heals more than our bodies—He heals hearts, souls and spirits, too. These are the healings that will follow us into the eternal ages. These are the healings that bring the greatest gift of all—eternal life. My prayer is that you will know Him and His healing power in life-transforming ways as you press in to be as healed as you want to be.

Afterword

M any who have heard our story or read this book are interested to know what has become of us since the devastating accident mentioned in the first chapter. At the time of this writing, it has been over fifteen years since Robin was first rushed through the rain to the trauma center at Mission Hospital.

Robin's journey back from the brink has been plenty difficult but it has also been a truly miraculous journey of faith. Once she recovered to the point of being able to return to work as a nurse, Robin took a job at the same hospital in which she recovered from the crash. The work was demanding, often requiring that she be on her feet throughout twelve hour shifts. Nevertheless, she did well at work. Over time, co-workers learned about what she had been through, inspiring awe and admiration. So it was no surprise when Mission Hospital asked her to take a prominent role in their fundraising campaign. Her story of former critical patient-turned-member of the nursing staff really got people's attention!

Physically, Robin continues to cope with some physiological after effects from the accident. She suffers from some nerve pain and is restricted by her inability to lift her left foot. To compensate, she wears a plastic brace on the lower part of her leg and foot. In addition, she utilizes a cane when she walks in order to keep her balance. Nevertheless, she can do most everything expected of someone her age except running.

By far the biggest concern after the accident was the brain trauma she endured. There was no guarantee she would return to us from unconsciousness. Even if she did we were warned that she may or may not have all her mental faculties. But to say Robin shows no diminishment in her mental acuity since the accident is to grossly understate the case. In fact, once she was able to drive again, Robin enrolled in an intensive accelerated Bachelors Degree program in Nursing at an area Christian University. It took time for her to take this step. After all, she had not been a college student for many years and she had to drive through the notorious L.A. area traffic each week. Nevertheless, she completed her BSN in 2003. Not long after that she enrolled in a Masters program (MSN) and completed her graduate degree as well.

After graduating with her Masters, Robin shifted her career focus to teaching. Today, she is an Assistant Professor of Nursing and the Course Lead for the Maternal-Child nursing education program of National University. And – surprise! – she has just begun working on her Doctorate.

From time-to-time Robin continues to share her story in public. She love to give glory to God and bear witness to His faithfulness through her considerable trials, tests and struggles. On many occasions, her testimony inspires people to lay hands on her as they pray for her healing to continue. We have no doubt that spiritual ministry, combined with the medical interventions and the hard work she has done, have brought her to the place she is now in her recovery. And, at the cutting edge of our faith, we continue to believe there is more to come!

One day, just a few years ago, we received a call from a Producer for the 700 Club Christian television program hosted by the Christian Broadcasting Network. They were interested in putting together a short feature on our story for broadcast. We agreed and a few weeks later a film crew came to our home and interviewed us as well as others. One person interviewed was the Clinical Nurse Specialist in charge of the ICU where Robin was taken. More than most other people she knew how critically injured Robin was and the level of danger she was in. The completed video is six minutes long and is available for viewing online at the CBN website, on Youtube, and it is linked from my website.

Robin has undergone quite a few surgical procedures since the crash. Some were to remove hardware that stabilized her orthopedic injuries. It was fun to be able to stand in church one morning and shake the clear plastic bags that were full of the hardware Robin once had in her body as we praised God for His mercy and power! Physical therapy has also been an important part of her total recovery process. She's shown courage to do whatever it takes in order to get better. Each morning I do my part by helping her put on her socks, brace, and shoes. This has been our habit for fifteen years. I am truly happy to do this for her; and I can't imagine Robin minds it too much either. After all, what wife wouldn't want her husband at her feet at the start of each new day?

In addition to all these signs of improvement and healing, Robin returned to a high level of involvement with her children's school and sports activities. Our two older children have both married and our oldest son and his wife are now the parents of our new triplet granddaughters! Our second son is growing in his role at work and our youngest son recently completed his Bachelors Degree and is now out on his own. Meanwhile, our daughter has begun her college career in another state. Through all these changes, challenges, and blessings Robin has demonstrated remarkable faith, hope, and love. It certainly has not been an easy road but it has been a wonder to behold her progress. She is indeed, as one friend calls her, "the miracle lady."

The church we planted in 2000 continued as a traditional church for eight years. Then, in 2008, I led in a total reconstitution of our church to a Vineyard-affiliated house church meeting in a residential neighborhood. We simply call it "Vineyard at Home". It has been a great blessing to lead in this effort and experience the give and take of such a simple, tight-knit, and caring community of believers.

About the same we changed the modality of our church I began making a serious effort to growing my practice as a professional Christian Counselor. Now, I see clients as a Pastoral Counselor in two office locations, including one I share with my son, Christopher, a licensed Marriage and Family Therapist. I have also continued to write, speak, and teach in church settings, conferences and in other settings. Each week I send a free e-newsletter to a growing readership. This publication is called Gracelets. It includes timely articles on spiritual growth, personal growth, well-being, marriage and family, and other topics as well as a video that relates to each edition's subject matter. Those wishing to receive Gracelets may request to be included on the mailing list by visiting BillFaris.com.

As you will note, much has transpired since I first began to engage the question How Healed Do You Want to Be? all those years ago. In spite of the challenges of living, life has definitely been worthwhile since I responded with an open heart to God's invitation to healing. I can only imagine what He will do in your life as you do the same!

Bill Faris, MPC
October, 2015

NOTES

CHAPTER 7: REDEEM

1. Merriam-Webster Dictionary Online at: www.m-w.com/dictionary/redeem
2. Cloud, Henry; Townsend, John, *How People Grow: What the Bible Reveals about Personal Growth*, Zondervan, 2001.
3. Barber, La Shawn: nowwhat.cog7.org/Articles/DrugsAlcohol/LivingWater.html
4. Ibid
5. CNN online news at: http://archive.recordonline.com/archive/2006/08/13/business-mltaylor-08-13.html

CHAPTER 8: REVELATION

1. Ilibagiza, Immaculée, *Left to Tell: Discovering God Amidst the Rwandan Holocaust*, Hay House, 2006, p. 75.
2. Ibid, 95.
3. Ibid, 101.
4. Ibid, 106-107.
5. From essay entitled "Keeping Our Priorities Straight" by Dr. K.C. Lehman. http://www.kclehman.com/download.php?doc=129

CHAPTER 9: BOLDNESS

1. Price, Charles; *The Real Faith*, Logos International, Plainfield, N.J., 1972, p. 5.
2. Ibid, p. 33.

CHAPTER 11: COMMUNITY

1. MacNutt, Francis, *The Nearly Perfect Crime*, Chosen Books, 2005, p. 16.

2. Crabb, Larry; *The Safest Place on Earth*, W Publishing Group, Nashville, TN, p. 4

3. Ibid, p. 8

STUDY GUIDE

Chapter 1: Crash

Group Discussion Questions

All the life-shaking experiences this world throws at us profoundly impact our bodies, oppress our souls and break our hearts. They also severely test our faith in God.

1. What situations have taught you to trust God while growing up or since you became a follower of Christ?

2. What situation is staring you down right now in your faith walk?

3. Have you ever experienced God giving you the "gift of fight"? Has a defiant spirit of faith every kept you alive? Be specific.

4. After the accident, the author danced very little with doubt. This was not always the case with him. This time, however, he did not surrender to the situation. The gift of fight kept him and fueled him. What have past faith struggles—even failures—taught you that you could share with our group to encourage us?

5. Previous to the crash, the author had sought God hard for healing at other times in his life. He did not linger on the shores of doubt, but plunged boldly into deeper waters to find God. Therefore, he had something to draw upon when his biggest faith test yet arrived. Many voices of doubt and fear will attack when life hits hard. The author recognized that he was in a battle and identified his proper enemy. What does that mean for you in your situation?

6. When a crisis of faith crashes into our lives. we often have little or no time to respond. Often, we are required to draw upon early faith lessons and the grace that has come to us because of them. If we are

to enter into all that God has for us, then we must live in the understanding that we are not in ultimate control of our life—even when
things are calm. How does this work with you?

Personal Exercise

1. Read Psalm 6:2-4 and pray it back to the Lord. Look back in your
life to past trials. Recite back to God how you saw his provision and
thank him. Engage your war: Say the whisper prayer, "No matter
what, I will trust you Lord."

2. How is the enemy (the devil) trying to whisper doubt into your situation to defraud God? Are you ready to take you life back by asking
God to keep you in a ceaseless undertone of prayer? Will you begin
listening for how He may be speaking to you even now? Read Palms
118:5-9. Write it out on a 3x5 card and post a copy in your car and
bathroom mirror. Memorize it and store this prayer in your heart for
future times of battles for yourself and others.

Going Deeper Questions

1. When it's your turn at bat and you are being tested—what do you
do?

2. What is the biggest crisis you faced in life? When it hit where did it
send you? What would you do different now?

3. Some believe that because healing comes from God, we have no
part in furthering it in our lives or the lives of others. Does that
notion "put the subject of healing to bed" for you?

Chapter 2: Mercy

Group Discussion Questions

Feelings of helplessness are not confined to any time or place. Any of us can feel alone and distraught just as the lame man by the pool of Bethesda. The days ahead may call for greater endurance and more robust faith than you have ever before needed. Do you want *things* to change or do *you* want to change? Read Hebrews 11:1-6 and Matthew 9:27-29.

1. What have you done in the past when the healing you have been waiting for has not come when you hoped it would? What about this has caused you grief? What has wasted your time? What has worked for you in the end?

2. Sometimes getting help requires an "outside your family" perspective. Where else can you turn to get an objective assessment of your situation?

3. What have you learned about wrestling with that powerful and invisible enemy called despair? Explain.

4. If you could experience a life-changing encounter with God in just one area of your life today, what would it be?

Personal Exercise

Read John 5:1-15. Be honest with yourself. Get a piece of paper or your journal. Picture Jesus asking you this question wherever you are right now. Do you want to be healed? What is happening to you in this moment as you read these words? Try to set aside feelings of guilt or shame and stay with the sense of God's mercy there with you. What situation in your life would He want to touch right now that has caused you to adopt an attitude of distrust or disappointment in Him? How could today be different?

Going Deeper Questions

1. Have you turned down God's gracious offer of healing in the past? Be specific.

2. What people, problems, and circumstances do you use for an excuse too often? Why?

3. On a piece of paper, make three lists. The first list is "lies". The second is "accusations" you fear. The third is "excuses" you make. Share your lists with God. Talk with Him about each point and listen for His answer. When you have finished, have a holy moment with the Lord in which you burn or otherwise dispose of the list as an act of surrender and worship.

4. Use this brief whisper prayer to do battle against doubt. Say, "I will keep-saying-yes-to-Lord no matter what!" Better yet, make up your own!

5. Instead of continuing to pin your hopes on improved circumstances, a better deal, a measure of relief, a way out of the mess you're in, or the answers to your "why me?" questions, consider how your present circumstances could somehow bring glory to God and help to others down the road. Can you hear that question as it reverberates once again through your soul: "Do you want to be healed?" I urge you to put this book down now and give the Lord your answer.

Chapter 3: Choice

Group Discussion Questions

Overburdened as this world is with trouble and sickness, we need those who have proved God's sufficiency in everyday, personal experiences to lead us to the fountain of life. This chapter starts with a question how healed do you want to be?   In our daily walk, we will be victorious only to the degree that we trust God. God is the one who can help us if we ask.

1. What does it mean if you say "yes" to the more of the Lord's healing work in your life right now? Where does that question take you in your journey?

2. Why do some choose not to seek healing? What has stopped you in the past?

3. Mike's tragic story of a spiritual fall and all it's ramification on others shows a hard lesson about how healed we want to be. What do you think was missing in Mike's life?

4. The author shows how therapy was used to help him bear fruit in his spiritual life to overcome "sofa days of depression" and now integration into ministry. He even went for more education and training. Have you ever considered talking deeply with a counselor about your life and your need for healing? If so, how has this kind of relationship advanced God's healing work in your life?

Personal Exercise

Take a pad and pen and write out in a few sentences what is your notion of healing? How do you embrace healing as a process and an event?

Draw three large concentric circles on the paper. One circle represents your body—list your physical healing needs within it. The next circle represents your emotions and self-image—list healing you need in these areas within that circle. The third circle represents your spiritual life—the seat of your relationship with God. List your spiritual healing needs within that circle. What do you observe when you review your paper? Are there any connections between the issues from circle to circle?

Finally, outside the circles write the names of the most important relationships you have in your life (don't forget to include God). Do any of these relationships need healing? Do you observe any connections with the needs in the circles and the needs in your relationships?

Who do you need in your life right now to see healing furthered in any of these areas? Write their names on the paper, too. Keep this paperwork as a prayer key and feel free to add to it or adjust it over time.

Going Deeper Questions

1. Where do you most profoundly feel the need for healing in your life today?

2. Is there progress (of any size) you can build on or gains that you could legitimately celebrate?

3. How do the biblical passages found in James 1:5; Matthew 6:33; and Matthew 9:29 relate to your situation?

Chapter 4: Release

Group Discussion Questions

Many of us walk around with a bullet inside that we are expected to ignore, deny or just get over. The powers of darkness are invested in the notion of your leaving the bullet there to do its damage. Why do you think so many of us have chosen to live life as the walking wounded? What is the price of neglecting the bullets we have taken in life?

1. Read 2 Thessalonians 3:2-5. God does not want our adversaries to swallow us up. How can we employ the promises of God's word like a compass to show us the way "into God's love and Christ's perseverance"?

2. The author says that things that cause injury only continue to inflame our wounds until they are dealt with or removed. What have you learned about removing the behaviors that cause injury in your life?

3. Repentance is a key to removing injury-inducing behaviors, attitudes and substances from our lives. How does true repentance look as compared to pseudo-repentance?

4. What does the author say about true repentance that you can relate to? Which, if any, of his concepts of repentance do you find it difficult to relate to? Why?

5. Read Hebrews 5:11-14 and 6:1-3. Also read Ephesians 4:28. What light do these passages shed on the difference between real repentance and mere regret?

Personal Exercise

How have you noticed your Christian faith affecting your conscience? Is there stuff your conscience used to let you "get away with" that it won't let you get away with anymore?

Take a moment to allow the Spirit of God to examine your life right now and point out anything He wants to deal with that is continuing to cause you injury. This is an exercise that, if undertaken regularly, will spare you no small amount of grief and destruction. How will you choose to respond to what you learn?

Going Deeper Questions

1. What obstacles to wholeness have you accepted as "just the way things are" in your life? Perhaps you are dealing with a debilitating physical condition, a disease or bodily injury, childhood abuse or abandonment, or personal betrayal. Try to be specific if you can.

2. If you have been battling the relentless pain of betrayal, divorce, injustice, besetting fear, or other injurious maladies you may have decided that it is your lot in life (what some call their "cross to bear"). Have you given up on looking for relief?

3. If you entertain habits, behaviors, attitudes, or relationships that are sinful and you know it then you need an encounter with the One whose words can spur you towards a miracle. Take a movement and listen with faith to His timeless voice. Is God saying to you: Stay put? Take it on the chin? Buck up? Get used to it? Tolerate it? Or, is He asking you that question of questions: "Do you want to be healed?"

4. Although healing includes the removal of toxic things which have caused you injury, suffering and loss, it does not stop there. Are you willing to allow God to move beyond the symptomatic levels of healing in your life?

Chapter 5: Repair

Group Discussion Questions

The best place we can go with our broken hearts, shattered dreams, afflicted bodies, and tortured memories is to God. Each account of healing in the Bible acts as a signpost indicating, "God was here." His divine interventions interrupt our sense of normal, and point us towards the One who performs wonderful works by his power. Read 1 Peter 5:7.

1. Why are miracles important today? Without them what are we left with in this life?

2. Experiencing God in supernatural ways reminds us of God's personal involvement in this world. How has God shown up in your life in ways you will always treasure?

3. Compare Matthew 5:45 with Psalms 77:14. What comes up for you?

4. What do passages like Ephesians 6:12; Acts 10:38; John 10:10 suggest about the reality of spiritual conflicts? How have you experienced the reality of the devil and his demonic forces?

5. What impact has human will (the decisions others have made) had on your need for repair (See John 1:13)?

Personal Exercise

God's miraculous repair of our body, soul, and spirit is a recurring theme in the Bible. Write out what you have come to believe concerning miracles today. What happens inside us when we acknowledge God's power over organic, atomic, interstellar, sub-atomic dimensions in the natural world? What happens to our prayer life when we consider how He turns water to wine, calms a storm, or multiplies food for people to eat?

What impacts you when you consider the sheer abundance of God's love as seen in the New Testament and in the world around you? If you could become a conduit of that love, in whose direction would you first point it?

Going Deeper Questions

1. How might a view of healing as a "one size fits all" experience limit the possibilities of what God can do in your life?

2. Fast or slow, large or small: what miracles of healing and repair do what?

3. Can you "borrow" faith from others to supplement your own? How?

4. What lessons about healing did you learn from the Janice story?

5. Why is the healing of our image of God one of the biggest breakthroughs for most people?

6. If your faith is weak, the author urges you to learn from others who can share their stronger faith with you. Who do you need in your life like that? Where can you connect with them?

Chapter 6: Restore

Group Discussion Questions

The grief process includes the following:
- shock and denial
- anger
- guilt
- loneliness
- recovery
- disorganization
- volatile emotions
- loss
- relief

Grief is not limited to death. It accompanies other losses as well. Grief is the suffering that goes with loss.

1. What are some of the grief-related emotions you have experienced? Can you describe how you feel and express grief? What ways have proved helpful? What ways have proved unhelpful?

2. One of the most challenging times for people to hold on to healing faith is when loved ones suffer. It can be hard to remain steadfast in prayer when recovery can take months or even years. Witnessing a loved one's pain day in and day out while healing is slow or not in evidence takes a toll. How can one stay present to the sufferer through surgeries, physical therapy, numerous doctor visits, and the like? What practical and spiritual lessons about how to cope could you share with others?

3. Have you ever offered silent prayer over someone close to you when they are not aware of it? Have you ever laid healing hands on your spouse, children or friend while they were asleep or otherwise unaware? What insights has God given you during such times? Share one of your stories.

4. Many times the aftermath of an accident forever changes the lives of those affected by it. Some deal with the heartache of knowing that they have lost things precious to them because of the actions or choices of others. Some deal with the guilt of knowing their own choices and behaviors have resulted in loss. A healthy sort of grief can be a friend when losses occur—whatever the cause. What are some things that distinguish a healthy grief response from an unhealthy one?

Personal Exercise

Praying "in the Holy Spirit" (I Corinthians 14: 14, 15; Jude verse 20) is one way to stay connected to God when life doesn't "make sense". When you don't know what to pray for specifically, it is important to choose to hold those in need of prayer before the Lord anyway. Many have found that praying in an unknown tongue—in words given by the Spirit—provides an especially valuable coping mechanism. There are other times when silently praying over people and reflecting on God's promises in Scripture may be appropriate as well. Read Romans 8:23-30; 2 Corinthians 4:6-18; 2Cor. 5:1-10. Try paraphrasing these passages in your journal as a prayer you can offer to God on behalf of those you love.

Going Deeper Questions

1. The author fought reversals and negativity by expressing thanks for the little mercies and the smallest of miracles wherever they might show up. Learning to give thanks is a fundamental aspect of faith. Try making a list of your blessings as if you were doing it for the very first time. How does doing so affect your mood? Your faith? Your interactions with God and others?

2. "Why?" questions haunt all of us. Becoming too focused on the "why?" questions can work against our recovery time, pain management, and overall restoration. The author suggests that one way out

of the "why?" conundrum involves focusing on the presence of God instead of the logical answers to "why?" Other escapes from the "why?" maze include showing gratitude, reaching out to others and becoming focused beyond the self.

3. The Bible insists that the harsh realities that rattle our sense of connection with God are ultimately not strong enough to truly shut him out. What promises can you adopt for yourself after reading 2 Timothy 2:13; Romans 8:35-39?

4. What are some areas in your life that require further restoration? Is it your bodily health, your spiritual health, your emotional well being, your personal relationships? Be specific as possible.

5. Who do you need to allow into the trials, struggles and hardships you are facing as a partner in your restoration?

6. How has giving yourself away in the past invited the healing process into you?

Chapter 7: Redeem

Group Discussion Questions

1. What does Bethany Hamilton's story say to you for the situation you find yourself in right now?

2. What has God allowed in your life so that you might glorify Him?

3. Look up Luke 22:31-32. If you were Simon in verse 31 and Jesus said to you, "Satan has asked to sift you as wheat. But I have prayed for you, that your faith may not fail." How would you respond?

4. In what ways do you feel like evil is trying to drive you down?

5. How do you counter Satan's ways for getting you down? What is not working and what is working?

Personal Exercise

One of the secrets of Bethany's life was she never stopped to let pity drowned her. She kept moving forward. The "why me" questions were kept in place. Instead, she fed her mind with "This was God's plan for my life and I'm going to go with it." This is what stories of redemption do. To redeem is to buy back, repurchase, win back. If humans can turn garbage into fuel, imagine what God can do with our errors, mistakes, tragedies, deficiencies, and sins. Make a detailed list the things in life God has redeemed in your life. Make a list of things God still wants to redeem in your life. Find one spiritual mentor in your life you can trust and go and ask them for help on how to redeem the things God has asked for.

Going Deeper Questions

1. God has a long history of turning our messes into messages, our trials into triumphs and our tests into testimonies. What is one of your stories you can tell someone who does not know Christ today about how he has redeemed your life?

2. What does God want to teach you right now as you read Ephesians 2:8-10 about your life?

3. Read Romans 5:1-5 what does it say about how to plug into God's mercy and healing grace?

4. What incident in your life can you look back on and see the truth of Romans 5:3-5?

5. How has Satan tried to use your physical illnesses, bodily deficits, emotional struggles or personal problems to threaten to disqualify you from being used by God or living a victorious life? Read the following promise afresh from the voice of your redeemer in Joel 2:25-27.

Chapter 8: Revelation

Group Discussion Questions

1. What impresses you about Immaculée's story?

2. Immaculée chose to embrace the reality that was in front of her instead of denying or resisting it. What posture do you take towards unwanted or unexpected events? What can you learn from Immaculée's example?

3. When we spend energy on resisting the reality of difficult situations, the resulting denial can hinder the potential for God to bring about profound changes in us. While Immaculée did not praise the circumstances in and of themselves, she was able to thank God for them because of how God used them to propel her deeper into Him. How might you apply this point-of-view to your own life experience?

4. How does the author speaks of the rare "level five" healing in this chapter?

5. Why do you think the author believes this "level five" healing it relatively rare?

6. Why is "level five" healing only available to people of faith who embrace their defeats, weaknesses, limitations, betrayals and limitations?

Personal Exercise

Believers through the ages have testified to the fact that God works in our weakness as well as in our strengths. Have you ever noticed how powerful it can be when we share our weaknesses and struggles with each other in a Christ-centered environment? Somehow, it seems God uses such occasions to mysteriously minister to us and through us.

Of course, we often instinctively resist embracing weakness at first. Perhaps this is because we would rather look better than plumb the possibilities for spiritual growth. Immaculée's story reminds us of what is possible when "looking good" is no longer an issue.

In light of these things, try writing a personal reflection on Augustine' quote: "In my deepest wound I saw Your glory—and it dazzled me." What does that statement mean to you? Where does it apply to your life experience?

Do the same with the author's quote: "We can take the healing and run, or we can approach our need for healing as an opportunity to better know our Healer."

Going Deeper Questions

1. Read Psalms 92. What does God want to say to you about your situation today?

2. Read Philippians 1:6. How does God bring about that process of change in you? Glance through the rest of Philippians and see what else Paul teaches us about change.

3. Read Romans 8:28. Nowhere in this passage does Paul claim that all things are good (in and of themselves). Instead, where does he put his confidence?

4. Read 2 Corinthians 12:10. Sometimes it seems we have been chosen to experience injustices we would never choose for ourselves. What are our choices when such times befall us?

5. Some popular theologies seem to pit faith against suffering and leave them unreconciled. How would you summarize your theology of suffering?

6. Do you agree with the author when he asserts that a good theology of healing requires us to also have a good theology of suffering? Why or why not?

7. Read the last part of this chapter ("the invitation") out loud and reflect on the questions posed at the end.

Chapter 9: Boldness

Group Discussion Questions

1. Have feelings of shame, fear or unimportance kept you from asking God for healing?

2. Is there something for which you have felt unable to be forgiven? How might this impact your potential to be healed?

3. Share one thing you learn from Matthew 7:7-8 with regard to prayer.

4. What is the difference between bold faith and foolish presumption? Can you identify an experience in which you have experienced one or the other?

Personal Exercise

Pray to God as if He were sitting right next to you. Talk to him about your pain, your experiences and in what ways you want to be healed. Be as real and unedited in pouring out your heart and emotions -- even anger or bitterness.

When you are finished, wait quietly for how God may respond to you. Be open to His assurance of forgiveness, His power and His healing touch on your heart and/or body. Thank Him for any blessing you experience and ask for more until you feel like it is done for now. Most importantly share with God where you are at and where you would like to be and ask Him to take you there.

Going Deeper Questions

1. Read Hebrews 4: 16. What distinct images does the term "throne of grace" bring up for you?

2. Throughout Hebrews, Chapter Four, Jesus Christ is described as our "High Priest". What are some of the things this High Priest does on our behalf, as described throughout the chapter? How does the knowledge that you have such an advocate make you feel about asking boldly of the Lord?

3. How might you distinguish *presumption* from authentic *bold faith?*

4. In this chapter, the author includes a quote from Charles S. Price who writes of faith as an actual grace. How does seeing faith in this way liberate you from needing to "whip up" faith through your own efforts?

5. Print or write out the eight scripture passages the author cites at the end of the chapter and write each of them into a prayer of your own composition.

Chapter 10: Environments

Group Discussion Questions

1. Identify some of the simple factors that turned a restaurant kitchen into a healing environment in the author's opening story.

2. Have you ever had the opportunity to share God's love by praying with someone in an everyday setting? Describe such a time if you can. How did it make you feel? Would you ever do it again?

3. The author asserts "all healing takes place in a healing environment" and "anywhere can be a healing environment." Do you agree with those two statements? Why or why not?

4. Do you believe one must possess a specific "healing gift" in order to spread healing to others?

5. What is one of the most healing environments you have ever been in? What are some of the specific things that stand out to you about this environment that made it so?

Personal Exercise

Take note of several of the healings and miracles recorded in the Gospels and Acts. What were the specific places, settings and circumstances of these healing activities?

Now think about the everyday settings you find yourself in. How could you imagine inviting healing into these places? As an exercise, write about things you could imagine doing in the following settings that might turn them into healing environments (even temporarily):

1. Family Life (example: "giving my children a daily hug a verbally blessing them in the Name of Jesus").
2. A Workplace
3. Among the Elderly
4. In the Marketplace
5. In a Neighborhood
6. At School

Going Deeper Questions

1. In the Bible, healings are sometimes connected to "the laying on of hands" of other kinds of physical touch (Acts 28:8; Luke 8:44, 45; Matthew 14:35-36; Mark 6:5). Why might touch play such an important role in these kinds of healing events? What role might touch play in bringing healing to the everyday places of your life?

2. Remarkably, it would seem that churches are not always healing environments. What are some of the things that make your church (if you are part of one) a healing environment? What are some things that could be done to make it more so? What part might you specifically play in bringing more healing to the life of your church?

3. The Bible indicates that God's word brings healing (Luke 4:18-19; Proverbs 4: 20-22). How might getting more of God's word into one's heart and mind increase the presence of healing in their lives? What are some specific ways you could increase your interaction with God's word on a daily basis?

4. Make a list of three specific healings you might need—one physical, one cognitive-emotional, one spiritual. What might you do to specifically expose each of these parts of your makeup to a greater level of God's healing power? What are some of the environments that might help you with this in each case?

Chapter 11: Community

Group Discussion Questions

1. What are a couple of things the author seems to appreciate about the church? What are a couple of things that seem to bother him? Can you relate to his struggles with the church?

2. "The best people I have ever known—the people who have most inspired me and the ones I most want to be like—are in my life because of (the church). But it is also true that (the church) has also introduced me to the people who have brought me the most disappointment, the most heartache and the most embarrassment." Do the author's words here describe your experience of the church? Why or why not?

3. Describe some specific things God given the church that make a potentially rich healing environment?

4. Name some of the things that are common to truly healing relationships?

5. What are some ways you have grown from positive or negative experiences you have had with the church?

Personal Exercise

Write your own letter to the church. If you are unfamiliar with the church, write about some of the things that have kept you from more deeply exploring church life. If you have church experience, make sure and note of some of the positive and negative things you have encountered and how they affected you. What would you want from the church? What are some of the hopes and dreams you have about the community of faith? What are some of the "deal breakers" that would cause you to give up on the church (if any).

Going Deeper Questions

1. Look up the following "one another" verses in the New Testament (John 13:34; John 15:12; Romans 12:10; Romans 14:13; 2 Corinthians 13:12; Galatians 6:2; Ephesians 4:32; Colossians 3:16; 1 Thessalonians 5:11; 1 Peter 1:22; 1 John 4:7). What are some of the potentially healing actions, behaviors and attitudes you find in them?

2. Read James 5:16. Imagine a scenario in your mind where the kind of interaction James is describing is taking place. What does it look like? Who is there? What are the physical surroundings as you imagine this scene taking place? What kinds of looks are on the faces of those in the scene?

3. Have you ever experienced a time when you have confessed your sins to another and had them pray over you for healing? Have you ever heard the confession of another person and prayed over them for their healing?

4. How does the high view of the church found in such passages as Hebrews 12: 22-23 inspire you to believe that God can do great things when His people gather together and share their lives in community?

5. Author Larry Crabb writes: "A connecting community, where each member is joined together in dynamic spiritual union, is a healing community". Compare this statement to the description of the early church found in Acts 2:41-47. Now take a moment and pray for the church you identify with and ask God to release more healing grace into the midst of your fellowship.

Chapter 12: Roadmap

Group Discussion Questions

1. How have you answered the two key questions in this book:
• Do you want to be healed?
• How healed do you want to be?

2. Why is it important to verbally declare our intentions to seek all the healing we can?

3. What were the stacked "stones of remembrance" (Joshua 4:6-22) designed to do for the people of Israel?

4. What kind of bookmark ceremony, commemoration or other point of remembrance could you imagine putting into place to mark the beginning of your healing journey?

5. How many of the five dimensions or aspects of healing can you recall from memory? Which of them seems most relevant to where you are in your healing journey at present?

Personal Exercise

Once you have decided to truly go for healing in your life, identify someone you can tell and ask for their support, prayers, encouragement and accountability. Be specific in regards to your healing needs and goals. Give them enough information to become a truly significant partner in your progress. Make sure and put your commitment to healing in writing and read it out loud to those who have accepted a partnership role in your healing. Allow time for feedback and clarification. Finally, have these people join you in signing and dating your written healing declaration.

Going Deeper Questions

1. When reviewing the lives of many of our Bible heroes, we see starts and stops, successes and reversals, accomplishments and defeats. How does this shape your own expectations of your healing journey ahead?

2. The author writes of a "vanguard" or "cutting edge" of faith—a high risk/high reward zone. What observations do you make about this cutting edge when you read the following passages from Hebrews, Chapter 11 concerning: Noah (Hebrews 11:7); Abraham (Hebrews 11:8-10) and Sarah (Hebrews 11:11)?

3. Given where you are on your "roadmap" at present, what does the next step of progress look like for you (be as specific as you can)? Would you say that it is more a matter of *removing* something? *Repair? Restoration? Redemption? Revelation?* Who or what do you need in your life right now to help you into that next step? Again, be as specific as possible.

About the Author

William T. "Bill" Faris, MPC has been a professional pastor, counselor and writer throughout his adult life. Currently, Bill is a part of the professional counseling staff of Marriage and Family Matters in Mission Viejo, California. In addition, he serves as the Director of the Vineyard Community Mission Network (VCMN), a network of house churches based in Orange County, CA that is affiliated with Vineyard USA.

Bill and Robin, a gifted nurse, have been married for over 30 years and have four children.

WHAT NOW?

To personally dig deeper, or to take your group through an expanded learning experience of **How Healed Do You Want to Be**, visit **HowHealed.com** and take the J-Log course online. This interactive study allows readers to engage further with the material and to interact in a larger online community.

To schedule Bill for speaking engagements or connect with his ministry, visit his website at www.HowHealed.com